GO! Evangelism
So Simple, Yet So Powerful!

fu: The Author,
Spencer Cho

GO! Evangelism
So Simple, Yet So Powerful!

Spencer Cho

gatekeeper press™
Tampa, Florida

GO! Evangelism: So Simple, Yet So Powerful Evangelism

Published by Gatekeeper Press
7853 Gunn Hwy., Suite 209
Tampa, FL 33626
www.GatekeeperPress.com

Library of Congress Control Number: 2022950542

ISBN (paperback): 9781662933585
eISBN: 9781662933592

GO! Evangelism

So Simple, Yet So Powerful!

Plant Powerful Seeds of the Gospel

In Over Fifty Major Languages

Come, Let Us GO Rescue

The Countless Perishing Souls!

SPENCER CHO

CONTENTS

Introduction

GO! Evangelism is a new and powerful paradigm that challenges all believers to immediately answer the call of evangelism and provides you with the confidence to embark on the Great Commission.

This book shows not only our heavenly Father's anxious heart lamenting the reality of many helpless, weak, and hesitating believers lacking firm faith, but also His earnest desire for all believers to go out on the road with passion and testify the Gospel.

All believers who have experienced God's grace and have been born again through the piercing realization of sin and repentance have the burden and hope of actively witnessing the Gospel of salvation to many perishing souls.

Even if you are not yet born again, the Holy Spirit will awaken, sustain, guide, and strengthen your spirit in the holy and blessed way, so that if you obey, muster courage, and go out boldly to plant the Seeds of the Gospel in many dying souls, you will surely experience the joy, blessings, and glory of receiving the power of the Holy Spirit and being born again.

Spencer Cho, the Founder of GO! Evangelism Ministry, urges and challenges all Christians to boldly go out and plant the 'Seeds of the Gospel' to as many perishing souls as possible and pray for their salvation, as time is running out fast and His coming is imminent.

For though I preach the gospel, I have nothing to glory of: for necessity is laid upon me; yea, woe is unto me, if I preach not the gospel! For if I do this thing willingly, I have a reward: but if against my will, a dispensation of the gospel is committed unto me. (1 Corinthians 9:16–17)

With the passionate inspiration from the Lord, Spencer established GO! Evangelism Ministry, a non-profit Christian organization almost twenty-five years ago. With the help of many pastors and missionaries worldwide, the GO! Ministry has published GO! *Gospel Tracts, the Powerful Seeds of the Gospel* in over fifty languages, each about twelve to twenty-four pages. GO! Ministry continues its powerful work of training evangelists in many cities of the nation.

These powerful *Seeds of the Gospel* tracts are now available at these GO! Ministry sites below:

www.GospelTracts.org

www.BibleTracts.org

The mission statement of Spencer is very brief: To reach the countless perishing souls and motivate and equip all believers to become evangelists who are full of enthusiasm, joy, and gratitude. This has been the mission the Lord has entrusted to him, and it is what he always does most of the time possible.

God has given us the most powerful and effective method of evangelism that is absolutely necessary in this age. It is not individual evangelism or relational evangelism, which many evangelists have used experiencing many difficulties, but planting the seeds of the Gospel in countless lost souls believing in God's power of salvation.

> I have planted, Apollos watered; but God gave the increase. So then neither is he that planteth any thing, neither he that watereth; but God that giveth the increase. Now he that planteth and he that watereth are one: and every man shall receive his own reward according to his own labour. (1 Corinthians 3:6–8)

Obeying God's command to "GO! and Plant" means embarking on the road with unconditional love and the conviction to sow the powerful 'seeds of the Gospel' within the hearts of many perishing souls as we firmly believe in God's almighty sovereignty. This approach has been the strongest, fastest, and easiest way to evangelize, reaching many souls with joy and great enthusiasm.

Spencer wrote this book to urgently challenge and encourage all Christians to participate in this amazing salvation work of God, because His return is imminent. He also has trained and raised many GO! Evangelists in many different cities of the country to actively go out and sow the 'Seeds of the Gospel' with joy and enthusiasm that God is very pleased with.

Over the past few years, as Spencer has personally walked the streets and planted the Seeds of the Gospel in more than fifty thousand dying souls, he came to realize why he has been always so happy and filled with the growing enthusiasm. He became convinced that the joy and happiness he enjoyed was not something he felt with his will, but that it was the joy of the heavens that God allowed him to experience and the happiness that God gave him.

> The Lord thy God in the midst of thee is mighty; he will save, he will rejoice over thee with joy; he will rest in his love, he will joy over thee with singing. (Zephaniah 3:17)

GO! Evangelism Ministry has published over 12.5 million copies of the GO! Gospel tracts in various languages, and over 10 million 'Seeds of the Gospel' have actually been planted in the hearts of many lost souls all over the country by many fellow GO! Evangelists.

"GO!" is a simple and yet very powerful command with profound implications. For too many perishing souls, the gate of hell is blocked only by the obedient, sacrificial, and loving God-glorifying work of evangelists.

GO! Evangelism removes all possible problems and stumbling blocks of existing evangelism approaches and makes us listen to the Lord's earnest request. In other words, we must go out unconditionally and sow the seeds of the Gospel by joyfully obeying God's voice: "Go and Plant!"

In such a field of evangelism, many GO! Evangelists experience the power of the Holy Spirit directly and discover that they are being transformed into amazingly faithful servants of God.

Spencer wants to share with all the believers in the United States and around the world the secret and rich blessings of a happy and prosperous Christian life, burning with this great joy and thrill, gratitude and praise, and passion and sense of duty.

Now, Spirit-filled GO! Evangelists full of holy zeal, joy, and enthusiasm are springing up like wildfire all over the United States, and countless lost souls are now being saved by God through their faithful dedication and fervent love for the Lord.

Chapter 1: America, Repent and Believe the Gospel!

America was built on a foundation of Christian principles and values. If we claim to be "one nation under God," how can we be so arrogant as to ignore His commandments and still expect His abundant blessings?

In John 14:15, Jesus said, "If ye love me, keep my commandments" (John 14:15).

The Book of Revelation clearly warns us about turning from our sins. The apostle John prophesied of prevalent, deadly sins in the end times—demon worship, idolatry, lukewarmness, murder, magic arts and witchcraft, sexual immorality, theft, and refusal to repent. The context makes it clear that these are sins that will be especially prevalent among those living in the end times.

> Remember therefore from whence thou art fallen, and repent, and do the first works; or else I will come unto thee quickly, and will remove thy candlestick out of his place, except thou repent. (Revelation 2:5)

The United States is now again entering an era of extreme division and chaos over the right to abortion. Since several years ago, the equality law to protect the rights of LGBTI (short for 'lesbian, gay, bisexual, transgender, and intersex'; also used as an abbreviation for 'people of various sexual orientations') people has been promoted centered on the Universal Right, and the Christian community is increasingly concerned about it.

Recently, during the COVID-19 pandemic, the church community has been saying that at this time prayer is needed more than ever to restore the significantly reduced church membership and the reduced worship attendance rate. The current situation in the United States is similar to that of the early church; just as the early church achieved victory through prayer in the midst of many hardships and problems, if we pray earnestly, God's work, which is greater than any of our problems, will surely happen.

The most serious of the many serious problems at present is the lack of genuine repentance of our believers. Living in this difficult time, our children are in a state of spiritual confusion due to pornography, sexual promiscuity, and pretense racism, and all of us believers who see America falling apart spiritually should repent and pray. The very chaotic America and the world can only be saved by God, and it is time for us spiritually asleep believers to wake up and fervently pray together.

> If my people, which are called by my name, shall humble themselves, and pray, and seek my face, and turn from their wicked ways; then will I hear from heaven, and will forgive their sin, and will heal their land. (2 Chronicles 7:14)

The United States has now reached an unprecedented family, religious, and ethical crisis. It reminds us of God's breaking heart that has no choice but to vomit out this nation when we oppose God's will (see Revelation 3:16). In this sorrow that this country that once took the lead in missions around the world has now reached a point where God has no choice but to vomit it out, the saints must rise up and pray and evangelize.

> Therefore also now, saith the LORD, turn ye even to me with all your heart, and with fasting, and with weeping, and with mourning: and rend your heart, and not your garments, and turn unto the LORD your God: for he is gracious and merciful, slow to anger, and of great kindness, and repenteth him of the evil. (Joel 2:12–13)

> We then, as workers together with him, beseech you also that ye receive not the grace of God in vain. (For he saith, I have heard thee in a time accepted, and in the day of salvation have I succoured thee: behold, now is the accepted time; behold, now is the day of salvation.) (2 Corinthians 6:1–2)

If we guard ourselves in the Lord with true repentance, He will raise us up. Everyone, let's repent and believe the Gospel. Let's repent of idolatry, of acting according to our own will, of arrogance, of vanity, of love of money, and of falling into materialism. We are still enslaved by the media, immersed in the lies and fun of the world. The world's powerful media are manipulating what we should believe, what we should fear, what we should love, and what we should hate.

After John the Baptist was arrested, Jesus came into Galilee, proclaiming the Gospel of God and saying, "Repent and believe the Gospel."

> Now after that John was put in prison, Jesus came into Galilee, preaching the gospel of the kingdom of God, and saying, The time is fulfilled, and the kingdom

of God is at hand: repent ye, and believe the gospel. (Mark 1:14–15)

Jesus told them to believe in the Gospel, indicating exactly how they needed to change their minds. Mark refers to Jesus' message as "the gospel of the kingdom of God" or "the good news of God." It was good news that the kingdom of God was at hand, and Jesus was preparing His listeners for how to be part of that kingdom.

The majority of Jesus' audience thought they were already righteous and would gain entrance to the kingdom of God because of their association to Abraham and Moses and because they thought they were keeping the laws God had given to Israel through Moses.

In Jesus' Sermon on the Mount (Matthew 5–7), Jesus taught His audiences how they should change their minds and how they could be part of the kingdom of God. Their association to Abraham and Moses wasn't good enough, and their supposedly righteous deeds simply were not enough. Jesus explained that the standard of righteousness God requires are truthful internal righteousness, and they certainly did not yet have that. They really needed a savior, but only a few would understand and recognize that need.

Jesus proclaimed that the people needed to repent and believe in the Gospel because the kingdom of God was at hand. Unfortunately, Jesus' audience wasn't yet prepared for the kingdom of God, because they hadn't yet understood and recognized that they really needed the Messiah to make them righteous, or that Jesus was the Messiah. They really needed to repent and believe in the Gospel right then, because the kingdom of God was close at hand. Some really did change their minds about how they could be righteous, and they believed in Jesus, but most of them and the nation as a whole did not believe.

In the near future, Jesus will return to the earth as King, and because of what the Bible tells us about the future, we also need to repent and believe in the Gospel, for the kingdom of God is at hand. We must change our minds from unbelief to belief and recognize that we are saved by grace through faith and not by our own works.

> For by grace are ye saved through faith; and that not of yourselves: it is the gift of God: not of works, lest any man should boast. (Ephesians 2:8–9)

When we believe in Christ for our salvation, we are already transferred to His kingdom.

> Who hath delivered us from the power of darkness, and hath translated us into the kingdom of his dear Son. (Colossians 1:13)

What really happens to an unsaved person when the person dies?

We often hear at funerals that the person the service is memorializing is in heaven. Even if the person has never made a profession of trusting Jesus Christ as Savior or has never shown any indication that he or she was saved, many still believe that the deceased person is in heaven.

Many people believe that everyone goes to heaven when they die. The Bible never says that all are going to heaven. The

Bible clearly states that there is only one way to get to heaven, and that is by trusting that Christ's blood was payment for one's sins. It is only through salvation that one can go to heaven.

The Bible teaches that there is no other way to salvation than through Jesus Christ. Jesus Himself says this in John 14:6:

> Jesus saith unto him, I am the way, the truth, and the life: no man cometh unto the Father, but by me.

Jesus is not just a way, as in one of many; Jesus is the only way, as in the one and only.

> Neither is there salvation in any other: for there is none other name under heaven given among men, whereby we must be saved. (Acts 4:12)

No one, regardless of achievement, reputation, special talent and knowledge, or personal holiness, can come to God the Father except through Jesus Christ. Jesus is the only way to heaven for several important reasons. Jesus was "chosen of God" to be the Savior (1 Peter 2:4). Jesus is the only one to have come down from heaven and to have returned there (John 3:13). Jesus is the only person to have lived a perfect human life (Hebrews 4:15). Jesus is the only sacrifice for sin (1 John 2:2; Hebrews 10:26). Jesus alone fulfilled the Law and the Prophets (Matthew 5:17). Jesus is the only man to have conquered death forever (Hebrews 2:14–15).

These three words—"Christ conquered death"—define the most important difference between Christianity and all other religions. No other religious leader ever predicted his own death and resurrection. Jesus is the only Mediator between God and man (1 Timothy 2:5). Jesus is the only man whom God has exalted to the highest place (Philippians 2:9).

America claimed to be "One nation under God"; now it has fallen and refuses to repent.

America, which was built on a foundation of Christian principles and values, simply refuses to repent. We have shaken our defiant fist at God and removed Him from our public square and our laws of governance. We have murdered innocent babies and have defiantly and proudly flaunted depraved sexual behavior. In our schools and in our homes, we have indoctrinated our innocent children in the ways of Baal.

When the cries of those oppressed by racial injustice and severe hatred of heart could no longer be ignored, we simply refused to repent.

Remember therefore from whence thou art fallen, and repent, and do the first works; or else I will come unto thee quickly, and will remove thy candlestick out of his place, except thou repent. (Revelation 2:5)

God is loving and merciful. But God is also just. We must return to our first love and put our hope and trust in Him, and in Him alone. We must repent as God's people, because the time is running out very fast. We must repent as one nation under God. Only the Word of God can save fallen humanity before it gets too late. Why America must repent communicates crucial and critical messages about repentance and its relevance and importance in today's society. Repenting and understanding the love of God is the absolute best and only way to reconcile with God.

> Ah sinful nation, a people laden with iniquity, a seed of evildoers, children that are corrupters: they have forsaken the Lord, they have provoked the Holy One of Israel unto anger, they are gone away backward. (Isaiah 1:4)

> Hear the word of the Lord, ye rulers of Sodom; give ear unto the law of our God, Ye people of Gomorrah. (Isaiah 1:10)

> And when ye spread forth your hands, I will hide mine eyes from you: yea, when ye make many prayers, I will not hear: your hands are full of blood. Wash you, make you clean; put away the evil of your doings from before mine eyes; cease to do evil; learn to do well; seek judgment, relieve the oppressed, judge the fatherless, plead for the widow. (Isaiah 1:15–17)

> If ye be willing and obedient, ye shall eat the good of the land. (Isaiah 1:19)

The Bible tells us that calling evil good and good evil will bring disaster on all those who do it.

> Woe unto them that call evil good, and good evil; that put darkness for light, and light for darkness; that put bitter for sweet, and sweet for bitter! (Isaiah 5:20)

> For the wrath of God is revealed from heaven against all ungodliness and unrighteousness of men, who hold the truth in unrighteousness. (Romans 1:18)

Being filled with all unrighteousness, fornication, wickedness, covetousness, maliciousness; full of envy, murder, debate, deceit, malignity; whisperers, backbiters, haters of God, despiteful, proud, boasters, inventors of evil things, disobedient to parents, without understanding, covenantbreakers, without natural affection, implacable, unmerciful: who knowing the judgment of God, that they which commit such things are worthy of death, not only do the same, but have pleasure in them that do them. (Romans 1:29–32)

We must come now and gather before the Lord to repent and pray and seek His face.

If my people, which are called by my name, shall humble themselves, and pray, and seek my face, and turn from their wicked ways; then will I hear from heaven, and will forgive their sin, and will heal their land. (2 Chronicles 7:14)

GO! Evangelism is Jonah's evangelism!

The saints who long for the Lord's imminent return and wait for Him are living in a special and urgent time now. The great commission that the Lord has entrusted and willed to Christians for them to preach the Gospel to all nations in the world seems to be nearing its fulfillment.

As the Lord said, "And this gospel of the kingdom shall be preached in all the world for a witness unto all nations; and then shall the end come" (Matthew 24:14). Now we feel the sense of urgency that we are living in the time when the Lord's return in the air is not far away.

However, at the same time, as I have personally met and witnessed the Gospel to more than fifty thousand multiracial souls over the past few years, I felt indescribable despair and sadness.

This is because I have come to the conclusion that it is absolutely impossible for the Gospel of salvation to be witnessed to countless perishing unbelievers around the world with the current slow, reluctant, and powerless evangelism paradigm.

Currently, most of the unreached people groups are regions with strong Hinduism, Sikhism, and Muslim traditions, where it seems almost impossible for the Gospel to enter; regions where it is difficult for missionaries to enter, such as Tibet; and regions that are politically difficult, such as North Korea and Iran. We need to spread the Gospel to these people as soon as possible, but if we depend only on the frontline missionaries and continue to live a selfish life of faith, saying, "It's good here," while resting in the walls of the church, the great commission will never be completed on time.

Let's restore the wildness of faith!

Now, all of us saints, it's time to have the heart of the Father, and in order to save even one more soul around us, we should not hesitate to face any difficulties, hardships, and persecutions, as did the first-century Christians. They risked their lives and boldly lived the lives of witnesses. It is time to restore our faith and carry the Gospel to countless perishing souls of all ethnic groups.

Even though we live in the abundance of the Gospel that overflows like a flood, the ears of the Spirit are completely closed due to sin, so we cannot hear or understand the life-saving true message. GO! Evangelism is a powerful new evangelism paradigm that awakens many poor souls who are dying in anguish, thirst, and hunger, and saves the world that is on the verge of destruction.

So who can save the world from falling apart and the millions of lost souls around us?

A person who has the thrill of salvation, a person who is heartbroken and overwhelmed just by hearing the name *Jesus*, a member who can confirm the miraculous fact that I have become a child of God: this person can restore this world with the Gospel.

The Prophet Jonah's Evangelism

We saints live comfortably in this secularized city that is flooded with the Gospel; however, this secular city is not a safe zone, but a city of evil like modern Sodom and Gomorrah. God continues to command, "Go, shout and proclaim!" but we all have become like Jonah, who disobeyed and ran away.

Arise, go to Nineveh, that great city, and cry out against it, for their wickedness has come up before me. (Jonah 1:2)

When Jonah heard the voice of God, he was very afraid and trembling. Despite God's call, Jonah fled away in a boat with fear and trembling at the people of Nineveh, who were on the road to destruction, arrogant, and rebellious.

Arise, go to Nineveh, that great city, and cry against it;
for their wickedness is come up before me. (Jonah 1:2)

When Jonah heard the voice of God, he was very afraid and trembling. In fear of the people of Nineveh, who were arrogant, rebellious, and on the way to destruction, Jonah showed his weakness, forsook God's call, and ran away in a boat. However, in the love that God compels, he achieved complete repentance and carried out the bold mission of an evangelist.

Jonah entered the rebellious city of 120,000 people, shouting, "This city will be destroyed in forty days from now" (see Jonah 3:4), urging and proclaiming the restoration of the city. The important thing to note here is that Nineveh was a very large city that required three days of walking, but he cried out as he went only one day.

As a GO! Evangelist, I have always wondered how many people would have heard the prophet's voice when Jonah urgently cried out, bursting his voice, while only walking for one day. The area I often visit to distribute GO! tracts is one where the crowds of shoppers continue to flow like rushing waves without stopping.

To every English-speaking person I meet on the road, I've said with a pleasant smile, "Hi, I have good news for you. Jesus loves you!" And to the Spanish-speaking Latino people, I've simply said, "Jesúscristo le ama mucho!" and delivered the GO! tract armed with the life-saving message in Spanish.

I've planted the seeds of the Gospel to hundreds of people in an hour. As I ran out of all the tracts I had in my carrying bag, I walked back to where I parked my car and prayed for the salvation of the hundreds of souls who received them. When I get back to the car, I pick up the second bag containing another five hundred tracts, and this time I walk on the next street. I continue smiling and shouting the name of Jesus Christ and distribute tracts to an additional five hundred people, sometimes answering personal conversations or questions. I usually plant the seeds of the Gospel to a total of more than 1,500 people for about three to four hours. What I am truly grateful for is that whenever I sow the 'seeds of the Gospel' to hundreds of people, God gives me an unbearable joy and an undying passion.

Jonah preached to 120,000 people in just one day.

If it was summer when Jonah cried out for repentance in the city of Nineveh, the capital of Assyria, the enemy country located in present-day Iraq, in the sweltering heat of up to 120 degrees Fahrenheit in hot summer, his sweat would have poured like rain and burst his throat. I can almost hear the urgent voice of Jonah, who must have cried out in warning of the judgment of God. I am certain that while the prophet Jonah was sweating profusely and proclaiming, "The judgment of God is coming upon this city," tears must have flowed from his eyes. This is because the disobedient Jonah had already repented and cried in the belly of the big fish for three days, and he would have the breaking heart of our heavenly Father, who loves the souls who are destined to perish.

Jonah must have cried over and over again with the heart of God, who has compassion on those 120,000 perishing souls. Jonah, who took the path of the fugitive out of fear, must have known all too well that if God's purpose was only judgment, there would have been no need for Him to send the prophet Jonah. Not only did he realize God's mourning and obey Him, but he also boldly entered the heart of the enemy's capital city with the same heartbreak as his heavenly Father and cried out that the city of Nineveh would fall after forty days. Even if Jonah, the prophet of God, who had been walking for a day in the sweltering heat, had cried out from 9 a.m. to 5 p.m. to burst his voice, I can think of four or five thousand people at most listening to his voice, based on my estimation.

But what is really surprising is that the work of repentance immediately appeared to all 120,000 people in that great city. Even the king of Nineveh got up from his throne, took off his robe, put on sackcloth, sat on ashes, and issued a decree, urging both humans and animals to diligently repent to Jehovah. Just like on the night of the Passover, when the whole of Egypt was filled with wailing and horror with unprecedented fear and surprise, the news of destruction and judgment from God's wrath spread in an instant to Nineveh, and all the people of the city paid full attention to Jonah, a prophet sent by God. They all repented and returned to God.

Although they were ignorant Gentiles who did not know God well and had no knowledge of the statutes, regulations, and laws of serving God, they humbly accepted the message of the prophet God had set up, looked back on their faults and sins, and repented. It sure was a miraculous event.

The way they cried out to the Lord and repented must have been the image of weak sinners who truly wanted to be forgiven, and God recognized this beautiful image and happily forgave all of them.

> Let the wicked forsake his way, and the unrighteous man his thoughts: and let him return unto the Lord, and he will have mercy upon him; and to our God, for he will abundantly pardon. (Isaiah 55:7)

Here is the true secret of Jonah's evangelism.

Jonah did not personally evangelize by meeting with 120,000 people, and he did not have a single Gospel tract in his hand. Jonah did neither personal evangelism nor relationship evangelism. He simply did not have time for these approaches.

When Jonah simply obeyed God's word, "Go and declare!" and went and proclaimed it, the Spirit of God opened the hearts of all the people of that city and urged them to repent. And when they obeyed and repented, God was pleased and allowed the work of salvation in that city.

The subject of evangelism is the Holy Spirit, and the sovereign of salvation is God.

If this is the case, is it really evangelism that Jonah just went out and shouted and proclaimed reluctantly? The situation in Nineveh was so tense that there was no time to share the essence of the Gospel and even less time to wait and see if they would repent and return.

Do you think the proclamation Jonah preached when he entered the city of Nineveh was really effective evangelism? It is the Lord who accurately defined *evangelism* and decided whether Jonah's act was truly evangelism or not.

> The men of Nineve shall rise up in the judgment with this generation, and shall condemn it: for they repented at the preaching of Jonas; and, behold, a greater than Jonas is here. (Luke 11:32)

> The men of Nineveh shall rise in judgment with this generation, and shall condemn it: because they repented at the preaching of Jonas; and, behold, a greater than Jonas is here. (Matthew 12:41)

The Lord clearly defined evangelism as evangelism, which Jonah obeyed and went to the people of Nineveh to shout and proclaim. He says that 120,000 people only heard the proclamation and repented. Even if our evangelists go and distribute GO! tracts with God's heartfelt love for the lost soul and the person of the Father who loves the soul, he says that it is sufficient evangelism that God wants and that he will save the soul.

All who were ordained to eternal life believed.

> And when the Gentiles heard this, they were glad, and glorified the word of the Lord: and as many as were ordained to eternal life believed. (Acts 13:48)

All the saints have received a prophetic mission to preach the Gospel of God and lead people on the path of salvation. Now is the time for evangelists of this prophetic mission to arise throughout the Americas and throughout the world. These are the prophets who understand God's longing heart, hear His words and prophesy, and announce and proclaim God's judgment to come soon. Just so did the prophets Isaiah, Jeremiah, Ezekiel, Nahum, Habakkuk, Daniel, Hosea, Micah, Zephaniah, and Joel proclaim and cry out God's judgment.

All saved saints must become Jonahs of this age who will open the gates of heaven and bring about the revival of Nineveh on this earth by planting the seeds of the Gospel to every soul they meet.

GO! Evangelists enjoy the life of a blessed witness.

The most important thing in GO! Evangelism is to realize that the field around you is the field of the Gospel to carry the GO! Gospel tracts with you regardless of location, object, or situation, and to evangelize indiscriminately to everyone you meet.

You should be longing to be filled with the Holy Spirit!

The secret is simple. All you need to do is to evangelize to save lost souls whom God is most pleased with and eagerly awaits. When you go to witness the Gospel by relying on the Holy Spirit, the subject of evangelism, and praying, you will begin to have close fellowship with God and experience the power of the Holy Spirit firsthand.

And my speech and my preaching was not with enticing words of man's wisdom, but in demonstration of the Spirit and of power. (1 Corinthians 2:4)

When the apostle Paul preached in Corinth, the largest, most luxurious, wealthy, and commercial center of Greece, he revealed his feelings that at first he was weak, afraid, and trembling greatly.

I also vividly remember how fearful, hesitant, and difficult it was when I first went out on the street with GO! tracts to be distributed several years ago, and I witnessed the Gospel to White, Black, and Latino people and countless multiracial people. In the busy and difficult life of America, I had a lot of work to do, but I only had negative thoughts about whether I could bear the fruits of the Gospel just by going out on the streets and sweating like this.

Although the life of an evangelist started like this, I began to experience the fervent presence of God as my priorities in my life began to change while I continued evangelizing to one hundred, five hundred, or thousands of people. One day, when the number of people who had received the seeds of the Gospel exceeded several thousands, the Lord began to touch my heart in a very special way.

As I was driving on the highway to return home after finishing evangelism on the road, tears suddenly came to my eyes. I cried and prayed for repentance: "Heavenly Father, I'm sorry. I have been living my life without ever understanding the heartache of my heavenly Father for so many souls who are dying like this, even though I say I love You and serve You.

So many souls are dying without knowing the Gospel. I repent of the past, when I could not live the life of the witness that the Lord so earnestly asked for and even showed me His will. Heavenly Father, from now on, I will live the life of a witness that You are pleased with, I promise!"

There were two things that I always regretted on the way home from evangelism on the road. First, how is it so difficult to meet a Christian who has been regenerated in this American land, which is a Christian country? And second, 'How come it's so difficult to meet an evangelist like this in this American land, where there are tens of thousands of churches all over the country? How sad is the heart of our Lord, who is looking at this spiritually dry land?

For many years, God has given me the joy and power that the Father gives to those who embrace the mystery of Christ when I pray to open the door of evangelism in the Holy Spirit and to open the hearts of souls who receive the GO! Gospel tracts in the Holy Spirit. I am receiving God's utmost attention and love and the amazing faith, freedom, and fullness that He has given me, which is clearly verified in the field of evangelism, and I am so grateful and thrilled. The praise did not stop.

The Secret to Rapidly Growing Our Faith

Another important secret that this writer has clearly realized while living the life of a GO! Evangelist is that if he does not plant the seeds of the Gospel himself in the field of life, he will never expect to grow in faith, nor can he live a life of walking closely with the Lord.

God did not create us to be content with only the things of this world. Our souls are revived only when intimate spiritual fellowship with our heavenly Father is established and continued. Only then will all the worries, anxieties, and worries of this world be resolved, and you will enjoy the true peace, joy, passion, and happiness that God has given you.

When you live the life of an evangelist who saves souls that the heavenly Father is most pleased with, you will enjoy the blessing of the Lord, who knows what you have not yet asked for and fills it abundantly. This is a blessing and a secret that only children who understand and obey God's heart can enjoy.

> For the eyes of the Lord run to and fro throughout the whole earth, to shew himself strong in the behalf of them whose heart is perfect toward him. Herein thou hast done foolishly: therefore from henceforth thou shalt have wars. (2 Chronicles 16:9)

In Acts 9, we see the story of Saul, who caught, imprisoned, and persecuted the disciples of the Lord, and how God humbled the arrogant man and brought him to a place of submission. If God can save Saul of Tarsus (who was eventually renamed Paul), anyone and everyone can be saved, as God wants all people to be saved.

> Who will have all men to be saved, and to come unto the knowledge of the truth. (1 Timothy 2:4)

We can see clearly through Paul's words how much he loved the Lord and turned into a servant of the Lord who devoted his life to the testimony of the Gospel.

But none of these things move me, neither count I my
life dear unto myself, so that I might finish my course
with joy, and the ministry, which I have received of the
Lord Jesus, to testify the gospel of the grace of God.
(Acts 20:24)

A person who deeply realizes the mystery of the cross in
Jesus Christ and is moved by the fact that he or she has been
saved, who now plants the powerful seeds of the Gospel of Jesus
Christ with determination and devotion to live for God as a
saved person, is the most blessed and happiest person in the
world.

The GO! Evangelist is going on the path of the most
meaningful and valuable missionary of God in life. In this age,
believers who realize the prophetic mission and continue to live
the life of an evangelist have true freedom, joy, and happiness in
life, as well as true peace that the world can never give. And the
Holy Spirit gives us the assurance that we will be the final victors
on the glorious day when the Lord comes.

Holy Lord, pour out the Holy Spirit of grace overflowingly
through the devotion of the GO! Evangelists who passionately
sow the powerful 'Seeds of the Gospel' so that the history of true
great awakening and being born again may flare up in this age.

And, behold, I come quickly; and my reward is with
me, to give every man according as his work shall be.
(Revelation 22:12)

Chapter 2: The World's Most Urgent Mission

"Every Christian is either a missionary or an impostor."
—Charles Spurgeon

If we have done nothing for Christ in our lives, let us begin now the extremely important, soul-saving, and urgent work.

The distribution of GO! Gospel tracts, the powerful seeds of the Gospel, between twelve to twenty-four pages each, armed with about 1,300 words, in over fifty languages, biblically solid and powerful, is the first urgent thing to do as each minute, each hour, and each day, tens of thousands die without any real access to the Gospel message that would rescue them from hell and save them for God's love.

"GO!" is a simple command with profound implications. It is a simple yet powerful strategy addressing the staggering reality of terrible judgment of God. For many perishing souls, the gate of hell is blocked only by the obedient, courageous, sacrificial, loving, and God-glorifying work of evangelists.

The reality is that millions and millions of souls are perishing and will suffer God's wrath and punishment for their rebellion in sin. How many souls will depart this life to a Christless eternity before you finish reading this chapter? Time is short! Eternity in hell is forever!

Therefore, the world's most urgent mission is to go out and plant powerful seeds of the Gospel, distributing GO! Evangelism tracts to as many perishing people as possible before time runs out.

Consider these additional evangelism quotes from Charles Spurgeon urging all believers:

I will remember distributing them in a town in England where tracts had never been distributed before, and going from house to house, and telling in humble language the things of the kingdom of God. I might have done nothing, if I had not been encouraged by finding myself able to do something. . . .

Tracts are adapted to those persons who have but little power and little ability, but nevertheless, wish to do something for Christ. They have not the tongue of the eloquent, but they may have the hand of the diligent. They cannot stand and preach, but they can stand and distribute here and there these silent preachers. . . . They may buy their thousand tracts, and these they can distribute broadcast.

Lost! Lost! Lost! Better a whole world on fire than a soul lost! Better every star quenched and the skies a wreck than a single soul to be lost!

When preaching and private talk are not available, you need to have a tract ready. . . . Get good striking tracts, or none at all. But a touching gospel tract may be the seed of eternal life. Therefore, do not go out without your tracts.

To be a soul winner is the happiest thing in the world. And with every soul you bring to Jesus Christ, you seem to get a new heaven here upon earth.

There is no joy in this world like union with Christ. The more we can feel it, the happier we are.

We are not called to proclaim philosophy and metaphysics, but the simple gospel. Man's fall, his need of a new birth, forgiveness through atonement, and salvation as the result of faith, these are, these are our battle-ax and weapons of war.

It is of no use for any of you to try to be soul-winners if you are not bearing fruit in your own lives. How can you serve the Lord with your lips if you do not serve Him with your lives? How can you preach His gospel with your tongues, when with hands, feet, and heart you are preaching the devil's gospel, and setting up an antichrist by your practical unholiness?

I have no confidence at all in polished speech or brilliant literary effort to bring about a revival, but I have all the confidence in the world in the poor saint who would weep her eyes out because people are living in sin. I would choose, if I might, under God, to be a soulwinner.

The powerful Gospel message is for GO! Evangelists to proclaim to everyone.

How much time do you have left in your life? Death often comes suddenly and unexpectedly. Did you know that your spirit and soul are eternal and live forever after your physical death? The Bible teaches that we consist of body, soul, and spirit:

And the very God of peace sanctify you wholly; and I pray God your whole spirit and soul and body be preserved blameless unto the coming of our Lord Jesus Christ. (1 Thessalonians 5:23)

You must prepare for life after death!

Time is running out fast! Is there life after death? Are heaven and hell real? Do you really know what really happens when you die? Our Creator God reveals clearly what happens when you die. As you will see, God has a plan for all who have ever lived, whether or not they knew about God during this lifetime.

God created you, loves you, and wants you home with Him! God gave up His Son to save you and give you eternal life in heaven. Claim the Great Promise!

For God so loved the world, that he gave his only begotten Son, that whosoever believeth in him should not perish, but have everlasting life. (John 3:16)

You must prepare for your death today! Tomorrow may be too late! The choice is yours!

If you are not biblically saved at this moment, you are one heartbeat away from hell. Eternal punishment in the lake of fire is waiting for you with no hope of ever getting out!

Hell is an everlasting, burning place where there will be weeping, wailing, and gnashing of teeth, a place of regret, where the smoke of the tormented souls goes up forever, and they find no rest, day or night (Matthew 13:42; Revelation 20:10).

It's not God's plan for anyone to end up in hell. It is solely your choice! If you choose Jesus, you become a part of the family of God and go to heaven and live with Him in eternity. However, if you reject Jesus, you go to hell and live with your father, the devil, for eternity (John 8:44).

You must prepare for your fateful moment!

The Bible continuously warns us of the Day of Judgment. The Holy God of creation hates sin, and the Day of Judgment is approaching fast. Those who live without forgiveness will have no other choice but to face eternal damnation in the fires of hell.

The choice you make now will affect your whole life and where you will spend eternity. God says, "And as it is appointed unto men once to die, but after this the judgment" (Hebrew 9:27).

Is it ever too late to be saved by God?

No, it is not too late for you to turn to Christ and be forgiven of your sins.

> If we confess our sins, he is faithful and just to forgive
> us our sins, and to cleanse us from all unrighteousness.
> (1 John 1:9)

Can I really know in advance where I will go?

Yes, of course! However, according to the Bible, we don't automatically go to heaven. In fact, hell—not heaven—is our default destination. Only when our sins are dealt with in Christ can we enter heaven.

God has provided us an answer to the matter of life and death, heaven and hell.

The most precious gifts God has given us are forgiveness of sin and eternal life in heaven.

What must I do to be saved?

You must repent and believe the Gospel.

The time is fulfilled, and the kingdom of God is at hand: repent ye, and believe the gospel. (Mark 1:15)

When Jesus said, "Repent," He was talking about a change of heart toward sin, the world, and God; He meant an inner change that gives rise to new ways of living that exalt Christ and give evidence of the truth of the Gospel.

The Assurance of Salvation and the Forgiveness of Sin.

Saving faith is trusting in Jesus Christ alone and in what He has done on the cross for salvation rather than what you have done to get into heaven. The moment you open your heart to Jesus Christ and place your complete trust in Him alone as your Lord and Savior, God promises to forgive your sins, save your soul, and reserve for you a home in heaven.

In my Father's house are many mansions: if it were not so, I would have told you. I go to prepare a place for you. And if I go and prepare a place for you, I will come again, and receive you unto myself; that where I am, there ye may be also. (John 14:2–3)

Jesus paid the penalty for our sins!

Clearly knowing that we were sinners, lost, hopeless, and totally incapable of saving ourselves, Jesus died for our sins! Jesus paid our death penalty in full. Jesus was our substitute! Christ's suffering was once for all! Why? So that He might bring us to God.

For Christ also hath once suffered for sins, the just for the unjust, that he might bring us to God, being put to death in the flesh, but quickened by the Spirit. (1 Peter 3:18)

What must I do to be saved?

You must accept Jesus Christ as your Lord and Savior. You can never earn your way into heaven by your good works!

Believe on the Lord Jesus Christ, and thou shalt be saved, and thy house. (Acts 16:31)

Quit working and start trusting Jesus! It is not what you can do that will save you, but what Christ has done for you. You must believe in Him alone to be saved!

Can I know for sure I will go to heaven?

You can be 100 percent sure that you are going to heaven. God wants you to be sure!

The Bible says:

These things have I written unto you that believe on the name of the Son of God; that ye may know that ye have eternal life, and that ye may believe on the name of the Son of God. (1 John 5:13)

You can make that final decision!

When you stand before God's judgment seat, He will ask you, "What did you do with My Son, Jesus Christ, who died for you? Did you receive Him as your Lord and Savior or reject Him?"

Rewards will be given for faithfulness in your Christian life.

For we must all appear before the judgment seat of Christ; that every one may receive the things done in his body, according to that he hath done, whether it be good or bad. (2 Corinthians 5:10)

You can settle this urgent matter of your eternal destiny right this moment! It means asking God's Son, Jesus Christ, to come into your heart. You must individually receive Christ as your Lord and your Savior.

Here is a suggested prayer:

"Dear heavenly Father, I am a sinner. I am sorry for my sins. Please forgive me for my sins. I believe Jesus Christ died for me on the cross and rose from the dead. I trust Jesus Christ alone as my Lord and Savior. Thank You for Your forgiveness and everlasting life. Please come into my life and teach me and help me to walk with You day by day. In Jesus' name, I pray. Amen."

You can receive eternal life as a free gift of God.

For the wages of sin is death; but the gift of God is eternal life through Jesus Christ our Lord. (Romans 6:23)

You can spend eternity with Jesus in heaven, for He promised:

And if I go and prepare a place for you, I will come again, and receive you unto myself; that where I am, there ye may be also. (John 14:3)

The goal of our ministry is to mobilize evangelists for the most exciting and loving cause in the world: rescuing perishing souls from eternal suffering and bringing them into the everlasting joy of accepting Jesus Christ as their Lord and Savior. Because hell is real.

The World's Most Urgent Mission

It is really important for us to know not just who we are but also who we are in our faith life. There are people who live with a sense of unhappiness despite having the wealth and honor of the world because their identity is not clear. The reason we lose our purpose in life, get frustrated, and wander is because we experience limitations and exhaustion without knowing the God who is with us. It is also because we are completely ignorant of the fact that we will soon be judged before the Lord for our entire past life.

For we must all appear before the judgment seat of Christ; that every one may receive the things done in his body, according to that he hath done, whether it be good or bad. (2 Corinthians 5:10)

From the very first moment of creation, we have been in an inseparable relationship with God. We must come to know the following two important things in our unbreakable relationship with God.

First, I have a sense of calling: I am called by God.

Second, I have a sense of mission: I have been sent by God.

But now thus saith the Lord that created thee, O Jacob, and he that formed thee, O Israel, Fear not: for I have redeemed thee, I have called thee by thy name; thou art mine. (Isaiah 43:1)

We are chosen and loved by God.

That is why we must truly value ourselves and live as children of God with a high sense of self-esteem. Another important thing we must have, along with the sense of calling, is the sense of mission. Having a mission sense means that we know God has a clear purpose for creating us. Our mission is the reason we live on this earth. Because we have a mission, our life direction is set correctly, and we live as people with a clear purpose and passion. Among the missions given to us, the greatest and most important mission is evangelism to save lost souls.

But ye are a chosen generation, a royal priesthood, an holy nation, a peculiar people; that ye should shew forth the praises of him who hath called you out of darkness into his marvellous light. (1 Peter 2:9)

After the apostle Paul experienced the Lord deeply, he decided to live his life for the Lord to save souls, and he decided to dedicate his life to that life-saving ministry.

> But none of these things move me, neither count I my life dear unto myself, so that I might finish my course with joy, and the ministry, which I have received of the Lord Jesus, to testify the gospel of the grace of God. (Acts 20:24)

Evangelism that saves countless perishing souls is the mission that God considers very important and is pleasing to Him. God has promised to make all evangelists into the stars of heaven.

> And they that be wise shall shine as the brightness of the firmament; and they that turn many to righteousness as the stars for ever and ever. (Daniel 12:3)

Punishment comes when we do not evangelize.

The mission of evangelism to save countless perishing souls is so great that the responsibility and punishment that comes when we do not fulfill that mission is also very great.

> When I say unto the wicked, Thou shalt surely die; and thou givest him not warning, nor speakest to warn the wicked from his wicked way, to save his life; the same wicked man shall die in his iniquity; but his blood will I require at thine hand. (Ezekiel 3:18)

> For though I preach the gospel, I have nothing to glory of: for necessity is laid upon me; yea, woe is unto me, if I preach not the gospel! For if I do this thing willingly,

I have a reward: but if against my will, a dispensation
of the gospel is committed unto me. (1 Corinthians
9:16–17)

If evangelists believe in the power of the Holy Spirit and
evangelize today, regardless of the fruits that appear in front
of them while evangelizing, that person knows evangelism
correctly. Evangelism is a beautiful walk with God, believing
and trusting and entrusting the soul. Our evangelist's role is to
sow the seeds of the Gospel, pray for the soul, and continue to
sow seeds to countless souls with the belief that God will save
these countless perishing souls.

There is no joy and blessing like evangelism.

There is a saying in the Talmud: "Think every day as the
last day of my life, and think every day as the beginning of my
life." If you think that today is the last day of your life, you will
want to do the most precious and valuable work. Also, if you
think that today is the first day of starting your life again, you
will try to fill your life with the most meaningful things.

Whereas ye know not what shall be on the morrow. For
what is your life? It is even a vapour, that appeareth for
a little time, and then vanisheth away. (James 4:14)

It is the limit of our lives that we cannot see tomorrow's
work even an inch ahead. When our lives pass by so quickly, we
will all stand before the Lord. And we will be evaluated on how
we lived our lives on this earth. What kind of life should we live
if we want to stand in the presence of the Lord with joy? It is
to live clearly knowing what the Lord is most pleased with and

what He has valued most. The hope and joy of the Lord is the salvation of many perishing souls.

> For this is good and acceptable in the sight of God our Saviour; who will have all men to be saved, and to come unto the knowledge of the truth. (1 Timothy 2:3–4)

The earnest desire of God is for all saints to embrace God's heart and become evangelists who save countless perishing souls.

How to Become an Evangelist

In order to become an evangelist who bears abundant fruit of the Gospel, you must have the following strong convictions:

1. You must have a clear assurance of salvation.

> But as many as received him, to them gave he power to become the sons of God, even to them that believe on his name. (John 1:12)

> Jesus answered and said unto him, Verily, verily, I say unto thee, Except a man be born again, he cannot see the kingdom of God. (John 3:3)

> Jesus answered, Verily, verily, I say unto thee, Except a man be born of water and of the Spirit, he cannot enter into the kingdom of God. (John 3:5)

2. You must be sure of the hope of heaven.

> For our conversation is in heaven; from whence also we look for the Saviour, the Lord Jesus Christ. (Philippians 3:20)

3. You must have the assurance of repentance and forgiveness.

If we confess our sins, he is faithful and just to forgive us our sins, and to cleanse us from all unrighteousness. (1 John 1:9)

4. You should never be ashamed of the Gospel.

For I am not ashamed of the gospel of Christ: for it is the power of God unto salvation to every one that believeth; to the Jew first, and also to the Greek. (Romans 1:16)

5. You must have the mission you received from the Lord Jesus and the love of many lost souls.

But none of these things move me, neither count I my life dear unto myself, so that I might finish my course with joy, and the ministry, which I have received of the Lord Jesus, to testify the gospel of the grace of God. (Acts 20:24)

There is a clear reason why churches are dying these days. This is because the pulpit does not preach about heaven and hell. The church pulpit doesn't talk about heaven, so church members who are not born again are living in the illusion that this world is heaven.

Hell is not proclaimed from the pulpit, so the church members do not preach the Gospel of the life of Jesus Christ to the many lost souls around them. Anyone who does not believe in Jesus should clearly know that the final destination is hell. What we evangelists must realize clearly is that evangelism is worthwhile to endure even a moment of awkwardness or even outright persecution.

Pastor Bill Hybels said this: "All the while, I thought that a healthy life of faith is a balanced life of faith. However, that was an illusion. A truly healthy and pleasing faith is a faith that understands the heavenly Father's heart. What is our heavenly Father's heart? It is evangelism to save lost souls."

The World's Most Urgent Mission

The world's most urgent mission is to save countless perishing souls around us who are not saved and will fall into eternal destruction. Too many souls who don't know Jesus Christ are perishing every day and going to hell. This is why we Christians must get busy in spreading the Gospel to all lost souls, using this powerful Gospel tool. There is great blessing in leading countless perishing souls to Christ. The greatest gift that one can give is to lead a person to receive eternal life. The work of soul-winning evangelism is greatly fulfilling and most satisfying.

For this urgent salvation of souls, the Lord has given us the easiest and most powerful tool of evangelism, GO! Evangelism Gospel tracts, armed with about 1,300 words in over fifty languages.

The world's most urgent mission is to distribute GO! Gospel tracts, biblically solid and containing the powerful Gospel message to save countless perishing souls. Hand out GO! tracts, the seeds of eternal life, with a sincere and pleasant smile, and say, "Hi, I would like to share good news with you," or simply, "Hi, I have good news for you!"

GO! Gospel tracts, the powerful seeds of the Gospel in over fifty languages, are available at our ministry sites below.

www.GospelTracts.org

www.Bibletracts.org

And, behold, I come quickly; and my reward is with me, to give every man according as his work shall be. (Revelation 22:12)

Chapter 3: Too Many Perishing Souls at Stake

If God had immediately punished us humans at the scene of our sins, there would probably be no survivors. But God is loving and patient, waiting for us to return to Him.

> Or despisest thou the riches of his goodness and forbearance and longsuffering; not knowing that the goodness of God leadeth thee to repentance? (Romans 2:4)

> The Lord is not slack concerning his promise, as some men count slackness; but is longsuffering to us-ward, not willing that any should perish, but that all should come to repentance. (2 Peter 3:9)

> And rend your heart, and not your garments, and turn unto the Lord your God: for he is gracious and merciful, slow to anger, and of great kindness, and repenteth him of the evil. (Joel 2:13)

The Gospel is "good news"; it's as a song writer said: "It's the best news ever." "God is love" is an absolutely true statement. However, He is more than love. He is not only God of justice, but He is also God of judgment and God of wrath. All these are perfectly intertwined and perfectly conformed to one another with a synergy surpassing all our understanding.

Hell is an everlasting, burning place!

The Bible confronts us with this heart-wrenching truth: hell is real! Souls are punished there. It's impossible to escape, because it lasts forever. It's almost too excruciating to think about, since hell is an everlasting burning place where there will be weeping, wailing, and gnashing of teeth, a place of regret where the smoke of those tormented goes up forever, and they find no rest, day or night.

How many millions and millions of souls now suffer God's just punishment for their rebellion in sin? No one can remove thoughts of hell, as it is a reality we all have to face.

And shall cast them into a furnace of fire: there shall be wailing and gnashing of teeth. (Matthew 13:42)

And the devil that deceived them was cast into the lake of fire and brimstone, where the beast and the false prophet are, and shall be tormented day and night for ever and ever. (Revelation 20:10)

We should never confuse God's mercy with His approval. In all truth, there are only two kinds of people on this earth.

- Those in the kingdom of light, or those in the kingdom of darkness
- Those in the narrow pathway to eternal life, or those in the broad pathway to eternal destruction
- Those in the process of getting prepared for heaven or for the journey to hell
- Those whose Father is either God or the devil

The followings represent perishing people:

1. They hate the good news of the Gospel of Jesus Christ.
2. They refuse to repent and reject the good news of the Gospel.
3. They take great pleasure in wickedness.
4. They will live the life of all kinds of immorality.
5. They will not believe the truth.
6. They will love sin.
7. They will never follow Jesus Christ.

As born again Christians, we must be the happiest, the most joyful, and the most hopeful people on the earth. We ought to have no fears and no anxieties because we have been chosen in eternity past for eternal future glory and happiness.

The Bible clearly warns, "For the wrath of God is revealed from heaven against all ungodliness and unrighteousness of men, who hold the truth in unrighteousness" (Romans 1:18).

I tell you, Nay: but, except ye repent, ye shall all likewise perish. (Luke 13:3)

My fellow evangelists, God has anointed and empowered us to lead all perishing souls to His Son, Jesus Christ, so they may hear the Gospel of salvation. We must reach out and rescue those who are perishing in sin! Too many souls are drowning in the sea of iniquity. They are in desperate need of the Gospel of salvation.

But if our gospel be hid, it is hid to them that are lost: in whom the god of this world hath blinded the minds of them which believe not, lest the light of the glorious gospel of Christ, who is the image of God, should shine unto them. (2 Corinthians 4:3–4)

But if the wicked will turn from all his sins that he hath committed, and keep all my statutes, and do that which is lawful and right, he shall surely live, he shall not die. (Ezekiel 18:21)

Why should we bother with perishing souls?

We must rescue the perishing because we fear they will be eternally suffering in hell without any hope of ever getting out. We should want to do this because we have great compassion on them and also because it is our mission that the Lord has entrusted to us earnestly.

Rescuing the countless perishing is God's will.

God has anointed and empowered us GO! Evangelists to lead people to His Son so they may hear the salvation message of Jesus Christ.

Say unto them, as I live, saith the Lord God, I have no pleasure in the death of the wicked; but that the wicked turn from his way and live: turn ye, turn ye from your evil ways; for why will ye die, O house of Israel? (Ezekiel 33:11)

The Lord is not slack concerning his promise, as some men count slackness; but is longsuffering to us-ward, not willing that any should perish, but that all should come to repentance. (2 Peter 3:9)

How often do we evangelists weep over a lost and dying world?

Have you ever done street evangelism, walking miles and miles and meeting hundreds of people with a sincere and pleasant smile, saying, "Hi, I would like to share good news with you," passing out GO! Gospel tracts, the powerful seeds of the Gospel? You will soon realize that there aren't too many Christians out there.

My personal experience, along with our ministry associates' testimonies, are almost identical, as we could find only 1 to 2 percent or less reacting positively to the Christian evangelists. The 98 to 99 percent of the people we've met on the streets were either indifferent or even hostile. Some shouted, "I'm not interested," or "I have my own place to go! Don't bother me anymore!" The most amazing thing is that they already know who we are! Maybe they find inscriptions on our face as Christian evangelists.

A small percentage, only 1 to 2 percent, whom we are confident are Christians, greet us with their sincere and warm smiles, saying, "Hey, you are planting seeds of the Gospel, aren't you?" or, "Hey, thank you so much for your efforts! God bless you! I wish I had your courage! Keep up the good work!"

Do you see clearly the lostness of this world?

We can have compassionate hearts for proclaiming Christ, but we will only be truly successful in rescuing the perishing if we are filled with a compassionate heart and urgency to proclaim as they are perishing and dying in sin! They are truly in desperate need of the Gospel lifeline.

We Americans are under God's divine judgment.

Who in times past suffered all nations to walk in their own ways. (Acts 14:16)

God's divine judgment has never changed throughout all of history, as clearly shown to the people of Israel. Many times throughout Scripture, God's chosen people, Israel, would reject God's commands, and God would give them exactly what they wanted, which was a miserable life without God.

The people of Israel didn't want God and His commands because they wanted to live like the sinful people around them. Once the people of Israel eventually repented of their sin of disobeying Him, He would restore them to Himself again. However, the excruciating pain and suffering they had to go through to get to God's restoration was just too horrible.

We Americans rejected God not only out of school campuses, places of employment, and government offices, but also out of many churches. Our nation as a whole has decided to reject God from interfering in our daily lives.

Our nation has followed the path that is outlined in Romans 1:18–32. Because of the government policies and laws being put in place by the leaders of our country, God is putting us under divine judgment by allowing us what we wanted: a nation without God.

In these verses from Romans, God specifically tells us exactly what happens when God finally abandons a nation and His people. There is no doubt that our nation will be going through some terrible times under this inevitable divine judgment.

We born again Christians cannot give up; we must stand for the truth, for God and His Word, urging our nation to repent and to return to Him. We can't just sit back and go along with the way things are going.

We need to go out and spread powerful seeds of the Gospel to everyone we meet on the streets, urging them to repent and come back to the Lord.

The excruciating pain of hell that will last forever for the unsaved souls.

Unsaved souls go down to Sheol. Unsaved souls go down to hell. Through the parable of the rich man and Lazarus, we learn that this Sheol is clearly the bottom of heaven and is a place of suffering from which there is no escape.

> And in hell he lift up his eyes, being in torments, and seeth Abraham afar off, and Lazarus in his bosom. (Luke 16:23)

> And beside all this, between us and you there is a great gulf fixed: so that they which would pass from hence to you cannot; neither can they pass to us, that would come from thence. (Luke 16:26)

When Judas Iscariot sold Jesus, then repented and committed suicide, he went to his own place, that is, to the place of destruction.

> That he may take part of this ministry and apostleship, from which Judas by transgression fell, that he might go to his own place. (Acts 1:25)

Sheol is a word that appears more than sixty times in the Old Testament and is translated as 'Hades' in the Greek translation of the Old Testament. It is a place of extreme pain and flames.

> And in hell he lift up his eyes, being in torments, and seeth Abraham afar off, and Lazarus in his bosom. And he cried and said, Father Abraham, have mercy on me, and send Lazarus, that he may dip the tip of his finger in water, and cool my tongue; for I am tormented in this flame. (Luke 16:23–24)

What kind of place is hell?

1. The place where souls will fall from the glory of God and suffer eternal destruction.

> Who shall be punished with everlasting destruction from the presence of the Lord, and from the glory of his power. (2 Thessalonians 1:9)

2. A place to dwell with the devil and his angels forever and suffer together. Hell is a lake of fire and a place of eternal flames.

> And the devil that deceived them was cast into the lake of fire and brimstone, where the beast and the false

prophet are, and shall be tormented day and night for
ever and ever. (Revelation 20:10)

3. It is a place of absolute darkness.

But the children of the kingdom shall be cast out into
outer darkness: there shall be weeping and gnashing of
teeth. (Matthew 8:12)

The dead souls of unbelievers go to Hades, that is, hell,
and suffer mental hell. After Jesus returns, their body and soul
together fall into the lake of fire, the second death. God wants
everyone to spend eternity with Him, but He also respects our
free will.

But whosoever drinketh of the water that I shall give
him shall never thirst; but the water that I shall give
him shall be in him a well of water springing up into
everlasting life. (John 4:14)

Anyone who wants can go to heaven.

But as many as received him, to them gave he power to
become the sons of God, even to them that believe on
his name. (John 1:12)

Jesus has already paid the price for our salvation, but we
must accept that gift and hand over ownership of our lives to
Jesus.

And he said to them all, If any man will come after me,
let him deny himself, and take up his cross daily, and
follow me. (Luke 9:23)

John chapter 1 shows us problems and solutions to problems.

He was in the world, and the world was made by him, and the world knew him not. He came unto his own, and his own received him not. But as many as received him, to them gave he power to become the sons of God, even to them that believe on his name. (John 1:10–12)

We can either believe in the price Jesus paid for all our sins, or we can choose to pay the price ourselves. But we must remember clearly that the price we have to pay for our sins is to spend eternity in hell.

There are too many perishing souls at stake!

We, the saints, like the apostle Paul, must become believers who do not stop worrying about the lost souls.

1. We believers must recover the tears for lost souls.

I say the truth in Christ, I lie not, my conscience also bearing me witness in the Holy Ghost, that I have great heaviness and continual sorrow in my heart. For I could wish that myself were accursed from Christ for my brethren, my kinsmen according to the flesh. (Romans 9:1–3)

For the countless souls who are not saved and are heading straight to eternal hell, there must be a repentance movement that weeps with tears and breaks our hearts. The sorrow for so many perishing souls must be restored to our hearts.

2. We must evangelize with confidence in God's faithful promise to the soul.

We must evangelize with the assurance that we will save all souls who repent and return to the Lord. We evangelists plant the seeds of the Gospel, water them with prayer, and evangelize with the assurance that God will surely save them.

Thousands of souls are headed for eternal destruction without hearing the Gospel. What are you doing?

Suddenly the Lord yelled at me. So many souls are going to hell—what are you doing? However, He says that among the countless souls heading to hell, there are not only unbelievers but also many saints who go to church, thinking that they have been saved.

Even if they go to church, they say they believe in Jesus, but they still do not have Jesus as their Savior and Lord, and they are living in their own way.

After believing in Jesus, you must put aside all your thoughts and theories and follow only the Word of the Lord, and you will be rewarded according to how the God of justice judges by the law of the Word. The Bible teaches that if you accept Jesus, you will go to heaven and not to hell.

> Examine yourselves, whether ye be in the faith; prove your own selves. Know ye not your own selves, how that Jesus Christ is in you, except ye be reprobates? (2 Corinthians 13:5)

If you do not have the faith that the Lord is very pleased with you and approves, you will fall into destruction without knowing it at all until you go to hell. The reason is pride and self-satisfaction. To those who are humble, the Lord gives them eyes to hear, ears to understand, and the grace that can lead to salvation every day, so that they will eventually reach the kingdom of heaven.

The following chapters will clearly show you step-by-step, "How can you have the assurance of salvation? How can you receive the Holy Spirit?"

And, behold, I come quickly; and my reward is with me, to give every man according as his work shall be. (Revelation 22:12)

Chapter 4: Why We Should All Become Active GO! Evangelists

B ecause evangelism is God's will, the Lord's great command, and the purpose of existence of the church and the saints, all believers must evangelize. Even if the Gospel preached through faith in Jesus is good news for the salvation of all mankind, if there is no one who preaches it, the church of today does not exist.

If you go out and do evangelism, you will feel and be convinced that it is not you who is doing it but that God is working with amazing power. Evangelism is our mission, but it is a wonderful work done in the extraordinary realm of God. Through evangelism the power of God the Father and Jesus Christ and the inspiration of the Holy Spirit are revealed beyond human means and methods. The apostle Paul said that God was pleased to save believers through the foolishness of evangelism, because the world did not know God by its own wisdom (1 Corinthians 1:21).

Because evangelism is God's solemn and urgent command to believers, evangelism is not an option given to us but rather a holy and solemn command of God given to us.

I charge thee therefore before God, and the Lord Jesus Christ, who shall judge the quick and the dead at his appearing and his kingdom; preach the word; be instant in season, out of season; reprove, rebuke, exhort with all longsuffering and doctrine. (2 Timothy 4:1–2)

Therefore, we believers must obey God's commands.

And I know that his commandment is life everlasting: whatsoever I speak therefore, even as the Father said unto me, so I speak. (John 12:50)

Our saints are living in the world now, but we are holy people of God who live before God. Our saints must now take the lead in evangelism to save perishing souls that accomplish the will of the Holy Father, the highest mission given to the holy people of God. All of the commands our Lord gave to His disciples when He ascended to heaven after thirty-three years of life were all commands for the salvation of souls. So why did the Lord emphasize evangelism so much? Because the purpose of the Lord, who forsook the throne of heaven and came to this earth in a physical body, was to evangelize me and you.

And he said unto them, Let us go into the next towns, that I may preach there also: for therefore came I forth. (Mark 1:38)

Evangelism means to share the good news of the Gospel of Jesus Christ. We've been given a great gift, and our Jesus Christ left us with clear instructions:

Go ye therefore, and teach all nations, baptizing them in the name of the Father, and of the Son, and of the Holy Ghost. (Matthew 28:19)

Before we can make disciples, we must first evangelize. We must first plant the powerful seeds of the Gospel to all the perishing souls around you that you can meet. That is the most powerful and most reliable way to salvation. When we evangelists sow the 'seeds of the Gospel' and pray for the salvation of the soul, our God opens, moves, and saves the soul.

The apostles call all believers to be involved in the work of evangelism, presenting the following two particular passages.

Walk in wisdom toward them that are without, redeeming the time. Let your speech be always with grace, seasoned with salt, that ye may know how ye ought to answer every man. (Colossians 4:5–6)

But sanctify the Lord God in your hearts: and be ready always to give an answer to every man that asketh you a reason of the hope that is in you with meekness and fear: Having a good conscience; that, whereas they speak evil of you, as of evildoers, they may be ashamed that falsely accuse your good conversation in Christ. (1 Peter 3:15–16)

The words of the Lord through His apostles are very clear. Evangelism is not simply the task of church leaders, pastors, and evangelists who are specially called, trained, and gifted. Every believer is called to be ready "to give an answer to every man that asketh you a reason of the hope that is in you" and to make the most of every opportunity (see Ephesians 5:16).

Live a mature life of faith full of joy and gratitude.

In order to live a mature life of faith full of joy and gratitude, you must do the following seven things diligently to grow as a child of God.

1. Pray daily.

Be careful for nothing; but in every thing by prayer and supplication with thanksgiving let your requests be made known unto God. (Philippians 4:6)

2. Read the Bible daily.

These were more noble than those in Thessalonica, in that they received the word with all readiness of mind, and searched the scriptures daily, whether those things were so. (Acts 17:11)

3. Attend worship service regularly at a church that teaches the Word of God biblically and is filled with love.

God is a Spirit: and they that worship him must worship him in spirit and in truth. (John 4:24)

4. Always love the Lord your God with all your heart.

Jesus said unto him, Thou shalt love the Lord thy God with all thy heart, and with all thy soul, and with all thy mind. (Matthew 22:37)

5. Live as a witness for Christ.

But ye shall receive power, after that the Holy Ghost is come upon you: and ye shall be witnesses unto me both in Jerusalem, and in all Judaea, and in Samaria, and unto the uttermost part of the earth. (Acts 1:8)

6. Have fellowship with those who can help you grow spiritually and in faith.

And they, continuing daily with one accord in the temple, and breaking bread from house to house, did eat their meat with gladness and singleness of heart, praising God, and having favour with all the people. And the Lord added to the church daily such as should be saved. (Acts 2:46–47)

7. Live a life strengthened in faith.

Rooted and built up in him, and stablished in the faith, as ye have been taught, abounding therein with thanksgiving. (Colossians 2:7)

In particular, prayer, the Word, and evangelism are very important in an individual's spiritual life. If prayer is the breath of our spirit, then the Word is the food of the spirit, and evangelism is like the active movement of the spirit. Therefore, no matter how hard one prays and studies the Word while living a spiritual life, a believer who does not put effort into evangelism cannot grow in a healthy and full spirit.

Evangelism should never be a burden.

We must know that evangelism is the necessary thing to receive all the blessings we desire. When our saints evangelize with passion, the abundant blessings the Lord has prepared are as follows:

First, we can obtain true spiritual food that cannot be supplied by the world.

Jesus saith unto them, My meat is to do the will of him that sent me, and to finish his work. (John 4:34)

These words were spoken by the Lord after preaching to a woman who came out to draw water from a well in Samaria.

What is the Lord saying is the Father's will and the Father's work? His will and work is to save lost souls, that is, evangelism.

Second, you can keep being filled with the Holy Spirit. Because the Holy Spirit is the Spirit who came to testify of Jesus, He dwells in the hearts of the saints who testify of Jesus diligently.

Third, we can receive answers to our prayers. The Lord said in John 15:7:

> If ye abide in me, and my words abide in you, ye shall ask what ye will, and it shall be done unto you.

The Lord's commandments to us are twofold. The first is that we love one another, and the second is that we love the souls around us and evangelize for their salvation. This is why evangelism is a necessary condition for answering prayers.

Fourth, it is to receive earthly blessings.

> But seek ye first the kingdom of God, and his righteousness; and all these things shall be added unto you. (Matthew 6:33)

Those who are diligent in evangelism are naturally destined to receive the blessings of this land.

The Reasons Why We Must Plant the Seeds of the Gospel to Everyone

The reasons why we saints must evangelize are as follows.

First, evangelism must be done because it is the heart of our loving heavenly Father. Through the sixty-six books of the Bible, what is the saddest heart that God reveals to us?

Have I any pleasure at all that the wicked should die? saith the Lord God: and not that he should return from his ways, and live? (Ezekiel 18:23)

The saddest thing about our God is that He does not want the wicked to perish in their sins.

Our Lord also saw the city of Jerusalem, which would be destroyed, and He wept for its souls (Luke 19:41–42). Whenever we meditate on these words, believers who understand the heart of the Lord receive a great shock. When the Lord Jesus weeps over the people of Jerusalem, who are bound to perish, it means that our God also weeps. To say that tears flow on the cheeks of the Lord Jesus means that tears also flow on the cheeks of our heavenly Father.

I meditate sometimes, asking, "Why did our Father, almighty God, shed tears for our wicked people who are bound to perish? Why didn't He mobilize the angels to spread the Gospel to the world through the two thousand years of church history?"

The Holy Spirit did not delay and immediately gave the answer. It is because our heavenly Father loves His children who believe and evangelize so much that He waited for us to give our evangelists a reward from heaven when they fulfill their mission to save those precious souls.

Even at this time, our God is so sorry that He shed tears for the countless sinners who have no choice but to be destroyed forever, but He is waiting for our saints to get up and go and testify to the Gospel.

Dear saints, if you truly love the Lord, you must evangelize. Also, we saints must evangelize because we are stewards in charge of the truth. Many lost souls around us are running towards eternal destruction. If we the saints do not evangelize even though we live the lives of stewards entrusted with the truth, it becomes a great evil in the sight of God.

As the Bible tells us, Jesus came so that we may live. Jesus wants everyone to know this truth so they, too, can be part of the kingdom of God. As born-again Christians, we do have good news, meant to be shared with everyone. The sharing of that truth—the good news of Jesus Christ—is defined as evangelism. It is sharing the message that not only is Jesus Christ the Son of God but also that He gave His life as a sacrifice for our sins. When we share this good news, Jesus ensures eternal life for anyone who believes.

> For God so loved the world, that he gave his only begotten Son, that whosoever believeth in him should not perish, but have everlasting life. (John 3:16)

> Jesus saith unto him, I am the way, the truth, and the life: no man cometh unto the Father, but by me. (John 14:6)

Every believer is called to become an evangelist.

Accepting that good news and then telling everyone about it so they know too is defined as evangelism. In the biblical sense, the word *evangelism* refers to the good news about Jesus Christ. So every believer is called to be an evangelist.

Jesus was very clear in His directives: We are to love God, love one another, repent of our sins, believe in Him, and spread this good news throughout the world.

If you met the One who is the way, the truth, and the life, then share Him freely and joyfully.

God gave us the following twenty-five important reasons to evangelize.

1. There is no other way to be saved except by trusting in Jesus Christ.

> Neither is there salvation in any other: for there is none other name under heaven given among men, whereby we must be saved. (Acts 4:12)

> Jesus saith unto him, I am the way, the truth, and the life: no man cometh unto the Father, but by me. (John 14:6)

2. The Lord strengthens and stands by those who share the Gospel.

> Notwithstanding the Lord stood with me, and strengthened me; that by me the preaching might be fully known, and that all the Gentiles might hear: and I was delivered out of the mouth of the lion. (2 Timothy 4:17)

3. When unbelievers repent and come to faith, they come to their senses.

> In meekness instructing those that oppose themselves; if God peradventure will give them repentance to the

acknowledging of the truth; and that they may recover themselves out of the snare of the devil, who are taken captive by him at his will. (2 Timothy 2:25–26)

4. When unbelievers believe and come to faith, they are saved from hell, and they know Jesus Christ.

For Christ also hath once suffered for sins, the just for the unjust, that he might bring us to God, being put to death in the flesh, but quickened by the Spirit. (1 Peter 3:18)

5. Witnessing is a holy calling by God.

Be not thou therefore ashamed of the testimony of our Lord, nor of me his prisoner: but be thou partaker of the afflictions of the gospel according to the power of God; who hath saved us, and called us with an holy calling, not according to our works, but according to his own purpose and grace, which was given us in Christ Jesus before the world began. (2 Timothy 1:8–9)

6. The words of the Gospel cannot be bound; they will do their work.

Wherein I suffer trouble, as an evil doer, even unto bonds; but the word of God is not bound. (2 Timothy 2:9)

7. If we never become obedient and proclaim the Gospel, we will be denied by Christ at the judgment.

If we suffer, we shall also reign with him: if we deny him, he also will deny us. (2 Timothy 2:12)

Also I say unto you, Whosoever shall confess me before men, him shall the Son of man also confess before the angels of God: but he that denieth me before men shall be denied before the angels of God. (Luke 12:8–9)

8. The good news of God's deliverance is glad news.

I have preached righteousness in the great congregation: lo, I have not refrained my lips, O Lord, thou knowest. (Psalm 40:9)

9. There are blessings and rewards when you are persecuted for proclaiming the Gospel.

Blessed are they which are persecuted for righteousness' sake: for theirs is the kingdom of heaven. Blessed are ye, when men shall revile you, and persecute you, and shall say all manner of evil against you falsely, for my sake. Rejoice, and be exceeding glad: for great is your reward in heaven: for so persecuted they the prophets which were before you. (Matthew 5:10–12)

10. God is glorified when others hear the words of the Gospel.

Let your light so shine before men, that they may see your good works, and glorify your Father which is in heaven. (Matthew 5:16)

11. Christ wept for the lost.

And when he was come near, he beheld the city, and wept over it. (Luke 19:41)

12. All non-believers must be warned about imminent judgment.

Whom we preach, warning every man, and teaching
every man in all wisdom; that we may present every
man perfect in Christ Jesus. (Colossians 1:28)

13. There is rejoicing in heaven when sinners repent and are
saved.

I say unto you, that likewise joy shall be in heaven over
one sinner that repenteth, more than over ninety and
nine just persons, which need no repentance. (Luke
15:7)

14. There is no other way to be saved from our sin and God's
wrath.

Neither is there salvation in any other: for there is none
other name under heaven given among men, whereby
we must be saved. (Acts 4:12)

15. Jesus Christ saves all who come to Him in repentance and
faith.

And it shall come to pass, that whosoever shall call on
the name of the Lord shall be saved. (Acts 2:21)

16. The gift of the Holy Spirit is directly tied to the mandate to
witness.

But ye shall receive power, after that the Holy Ghost
is come upon you: and ye shall be witnesses unto me
both in Jerusalem, and in all Judaea, and in Samaria,
and unto the uttermost part of the earth. (Acts 1:8)

17. When Christians evangelize, they are working with God;
now is the day of salvation.

We then, as workers together with him, beseech you also that ye receive not the grace of God in vain. (For he saith, I have heard thee in a time accepted, and in the day of salvation have I succoured thee: behold, now is the accepted time; behold, now is the day of salvation.) (2 Corinthians 6:1–2)

18. We share the Gospel because we fear God.

And I say unto you my friends, Be not afraid of them that kill the body, and after that have no more that they can do. But I will forewarn you whom ye shall fear: Fear him, which after he hath killed hath power to cast into hell; yea, I say unto you, Fear him. (Luke 12:4–5)

19. It increases thanksgiving to God whenever perishing souls are saved.

For all things are for your sakes, that the abundant grace might through the thanksgiving of many redound to the glory of God. (2 Corinthians 4:15)

20. Witnessing is evidence that God's love has been poured out in our hearts.

And hope maketh not ashamed; because the love of God is shed abroad in our hearts by the Holy Ghost which is given unto us. (Romans 5:5)

21. Jesus came to seek and save the lost, and we are called to follow His example.

For the Son of man is come to seek and to save that which was lost. (Luke 19:10)

Then said Jesus to them again, Peace be unto you: as my Father hath sent me, even so send I you. (John 20:21)

22. Those who preach the good news are blessed and have beautiful feet.

How beautiful upon the mountains are the feet of him that bringeth good tidings, that publisheth peace; that bringeth good tidings of good, that publisheth salvation; that saith unto Zion, Thy God reigneth. (Isaiah 52:7)

23. We share the good news so that all might glorify and worship God.

And that the Gentiles might glorify God for his mercy; as it is written, for this cause I will confess to thee among the Gentiles, and sing unto thy name. And again he saith, Rejoice, ye Gentiles, with his people. And again, Praise the Lord, all ye Gentiles; and laud him, all ye people. (Romans 15:9–11)

24. When we share our faith, God promises to be with us, even unto the end of the world.

Teaching them to observe all things whatsoever I have commanded you: and, lo, I am with you alway, even unto the end of the world. Amen. (Matthew 28:20)

25. God gives Christians great joy whenever the Gospel is shared.

What then? notwithstanding, every way, whether in pretence, or in truth, Christ is preached; and I therein do rejoice, yea, and will rejoice. (Philippians 1:18)

As we follow the storyline of the early church, not only do we see that the apostles sought to evangelize and disciple others, but we also see many ordinary believers boldly sharing the Gospel.

Consider this account following the stoning of Stephen in Acts chapter 8:

> And Saul was consenting unto his death. And at that time there was a great persecution against the church which was at Jerusalem; and they were all scattered abroad throughout the regions of Judaea and Samaria, except the apostles. (Acts 8:1)

Acts 8:4 continues:

> Therefore they that were scattered abroad went every where preaching the word.

They that were scattered abroad went about sharing the Gospel with others.

Two more important reasons why we should plant the seeds of the Gospel:

1. If we do not witness the Gospel, we have woe to ourselves, as the apostle Paul said:

> For though I preach the gospel, I have nothing to glory of: for necessity is laid upon me; yea, woe is unto me, if I preach not the gospel! (1 Corinthians 9:16)

The apostle Paul must have vividly remembered the following words:

> When I say unto the wicked, Thou shalt surely die; and
> thou givest him not warning, nor speakest to warn the
> wicked from his wicked way, to save his life; the same
> wicked man shall die in his iniquity; but his blood will
> I require at thine hand. (Ezekiel 3:18)

We must never forget that we GO! Evangelists are the watchmen of this age who must enlighten the wicked, that is, unbelievers, with blessings on behalf of God.

2. There is a wonderful reward prepared for all evangelists.

The reason why today's churches cannot revive is because they did not have compassion on the many lost souls and did not sow the 'seeds of the Gospel' to save them.

> And they that be wise shall shine as the brightness of the
> firmament; and they that turn many to righteousness
> as the stars for ever and ever. (Daniel 12:3)

If you evangelize, God will provide you with the power of the Holy Spirit, because the Holy Spirit is the Spirit of the Gospel witness. Just as He poured out amazing power on the apostles and evangelists who are active in the Book of Acts, He gives the evangelist passion and the experience of God's amazing power and work.

If you evangelize, God will give you amazing joy and passion. The evangelistic saints are filled with endless joy. Churches and believers who do not evangelize are dead churches. A church filled with joy, power, and passion is a living church that evangelizes.

We pray for the work of the Holy Spirit to open the hearts of all the saints who read this book and to open their ears wide to hear and obey God's Word so that they may plant the 'seeds of the Gospel'.

We firmly believe that when God's kingdom is expanded through evangelism, God's will is done through the expansion of God's kingdom, God's will is fulfilled, and God's glory will be greatly revealed in the whole earth and in heaven. In the name of Jesus Christ, I earnestly pray that you can participate in the harvesting of souls that God is very pleased with you and will give you all the precious and abundant fruits of evangelism.

And, behold, I come quickly; and my reward is with me, to give every man according as his work shall be. (Revelation 22:12)

Chapter 5: The Mission of GO! Evangelism (With GO! Training Manual)

Evangelism is the greatest spiritual privilege of all believers, and at the same time, it is the greatest blessing the Lord has given us. Therefore, we think that our Lord Himself set the example of evangelism and strongly commanded us to go to the ends of the earth to preach the Gospel, since He knew that evangelism is such a great blessing to all of us.

Among believers, there is probably no one who does not know this, but in reality, evangelism is a great burden and fear for many believers. GO! Evangelists are such burdened people. They are the ones who awaken the souls of the saints who are trying to stay in the spiritual safe zone with moderate compromise. These GO! Evangelists do not just talk, but they actually go out on the street every week to evangelize many perishing souls continuously and passionately, and they are the ones who challenge many believers to live the life of a witness.

GO! Evangelists are the ones who remind us of what is important to us and what comes first, as we receive the Lord's sorrowful heart for the salvation of souls in our hearts and work toward saving souls with all our passion. The purpose of this book is to challenge and awaken all Christians around the world to witness to the Gospel of salvation to millions of lost souls.

This book inspires not only the theory of evangelism but also the practical passion for evangelism. This is a book that allows the members who have always had a burden for evangelism to get up and move forward immediately. This is a book to save perishing souls, revive the church, and expand the kingdom of God.

I hope that the cry that the GO! Evangelists have cried and emphasized countless times will be heard as it is, so that the souls of many saints who read this book will gain strength and move on to the path of God's blessing.

Are you dreaming of being a GO! Evangelist on a prophetic mission?

The people most needed on this earth right now are evangelists of the prophetic mission who are burning with God's character and passion. God wants evangelists full of passion and love for the Gospel to rise like a fire to save the lost souls here in America and around the world. He wants them to get up and go, boldly proclaiming the Gospel of salvation to countless perishing souls who are desperately heading for destruction.

The God of love has established prophets in every age to accomplish the work of salvation for humankind, which is bound to perish forever, and He is still setting up prophets in this age. Mission historians have called the nineteenth century "the great missionary century" and the twentieth century "the greater century." The twenty-first century is the current century of the AD era, in accordance with the Gregorian calendar. It began on January 1, 2001, and will end on December 31, 2100. It is the first century of the third millennium.

We can now say that we are living in the twenty-first century, when the Second Coming of the Lord is imminent, and we are living in the last century of the greatest and most thrilling missionary work.

Acts chapter 2 speaks of a wonderful revival in this great last century.

And it shall come to pass in the last days, saith God, I will pour out of my Spirit upon all flesh: and your sons and your daughters shall prophesy, and your young men shall see visions, and your old men shall dream dreams: and on my servants and on my handmaidens I will pour out in those days of my Spirit; and they shall prophesy: and I will shew wonders in heaven above, and signs in the earth beneath; blood, and fire, and vapour of smoke: the sun shall be turned into darkness, and the moon into blood, before that great and notable day of the Lord come: and it shall come to pass, that whosoever shall call on the name of the Lord shall be saved. (Acts 2:17–21)

God wants all children, young people, and old people to be mobilized to be used as tools for the Gospel of God in this age. This is an urgent time when all of us believers must rise up and be used greatly for the explosive revival of the Gospel of Jesus Christ. We love God because He first loved us, even to give us His life. The saints who have deeply experienced this wonderful love of God cannot help but live a life that pleases the Father.

If you are a saint who understands who our heavenly Father is, what kind of love He has for us, and what to do for Him, then you will realize that what God is most pleased with is evangelism that saves countless perishing souls, and you can live a life that burns with holy passion.

I am a blessed GO! Evangelist!

I experience the love of the Father who rejoices at this evangelist, loves quietly, rejoices in love, and continues to have close and passionate fellowship with the Father. In the field of evangelism, I experience the power of the Holy Spirit, who always accompanies me, and I discover myself amazingly transforming into a man of God.

I am writing this book with the conviction that the history of going and planting seeds should happen to all believers who are enthusiastically following in obedience to God's call all over America and other parts of the world.

In many parts of the United States, these holy zealous groups are rising. Because of the burning passion for saving souls, many GO! Evangelists are taking to the streets to warn of the imminent judgment of God and urge them to repent and believe the Gospel.

With earnest desire, in downtown Los Angeles and downtown Hollywood, in Harlem Street and the subway in New York, in New Jersey, in Maryland, in Dallas and San Antonio, Texas, in Boston, in Tacoma, Washington, and in the port city of Seattle, we are boldly preaching the Gospel to the souls we meet.

We also proclaim the Gospel in San Francisco, Phoenix, Florida, and many other cities in the United States.

The United States is a multiethnic country where diverse ethnic groups from almost all regions of the world live together as a community with the characteristics of each region's culture. Therefore, America is a golden fishing ground for evangelism, where you can meet many diverse races and testify of the Gospel.

After establishing GO! Evangelism Ministry with this dream and vision many years ago, the author has been training and challenging believers in numerous churches in the United States, armed with the amazing grace that the Holy Spirit has given him, numerous testimonies, and know-how. In the meantime, I have seen evangelism to many multiracial groups that I could not have imagined, bearing fruit by tens to hundreds of people a week.

Therefore, through the GO! Evangelism seminar, we have been challenging and training the members of churches in other regions. GO! Gospel tracts, armed with about 1,300 words, in twelve to twenty-four pages each, are a powerful evangelistic tool designed by the Holy Spirit, translated into more than fifty languages and with over 12 million copies published. These tracts make it easily accessible to our neighbors of all multiethnic groups. We can't help but be thankful that the scope of our evangelism has been widened to the souls of all nations around the world.

I believe that God will grant all of our GO! Evangelists the blessing of being wonderfully used as the secret weapon of God's Gospel to complete world missions.

What is the reason why believers are reluctant to step forward?

The reality of all believers is that even if they have a desire to do evangelism, they cannot easily do so. The reason why all the saints are not willing to step forward as evangelists is the fear of social rejection. They also experience the burden of responsibility for the evangelism target until they are saved, lack of time, lack of proper evangelism training, and weak faith.

On the other hand, the spiritual complacency of being busy only in fellowship and activities in the church and not being able to approach and communicate with the unbelievers around is also a serious problem.

Why is GO! Evangelism so powerful?

GO! Evangelism is a powerful evangelistic method that challenges all of us to easily jump into the field of evangelism following the heart of our heavenly Father, who is anxiously waiting for lost souls. GO! Evangelism ignites the problems of existing evangelism and arouses religious enthusiasm. In other words, evangelism means obeying God's voice, who says, "Go and preach," and unconditionally going out on the road and planting the seeds of the Gospel. It starts with a simple greeting and a pleasant smile to all the souls you meet anytime, anywhere, saying, "I have good news for you! Jesus loves you!" All you have to do is hand over the GO! Gospel tract. After that, the person reads the tract, starting with questions, including, "Are You Saved?" "Where Will You Spend Eternity?" "How Much Time Do You Have Left in Your Life?" While the person continues to read the salvation message, the Holy Spirit will convict the heart for salvation.

Our evangelist's role is to sow the seeds of the Gospel in every soul we meet.

> I have planted, Apollos watered; but God gave the increase. So then neither is he that planteth anything, neither he that watereth; but God that giveth the increase. Now he that planteth and he that watereth are one: and every man shall receive his own reward according to his own labour. (1 Corinthians 3:6–8)

The GO! Gospel tract contains information about accepting Jesus as our Savior and Lord through the cross and resurrection, repentance and forgiveness, and the assurance of salvation through faith. Thousands of believers who have completed the GO! Evangelism seminar go out with their GO! tracts and witness the Gospel to dozens or hundreds of people a week.

You can also become a powerful GO! Evangelist!

The Holy Spirit will lead you and all believers across the country reading this book to become a GO! Evangelist, planting the powerful seeds of the Gospel in the many lost souls around them with joy, boldness, and a sense of mission. The seeds of the Gospel tracts are available at our sites:

www.GospelTracts.org

www.BibleTracts.org

God has blessed and allowed GO! Evangelists to plant the powerful seeds of the Gospel to over ten million souls over the past few years. As more GO Evangelists are rising like fire across the country, we hope and pray for God's amazing work of salvation that will be accomplished through GO! Evangelists who have been challenged and determined while reading this book.

America, the Golden Fishing Ground of Evangelism

America now is the golden fishing ground for evangelism. No matter where you go, you can meet and evangelize people of all races from all over the world. Many fast-food restaurants everywhere are good places to evangelize. I stop by several fast-food restaurants on my way to work in the morning, order a cup of coffee, and go around to each table, saying, "I have good news for you!" with a sincere and pleasant smile and handing out GO! tracts. If they ask, "What is it about?" I tell them the truth. "It is a Gospel tract. It will show you how to get to heaven." Sometimes we meet enemies of the Gospel, but we pray earnestly with our dignity as an ambassador of the Gospel of the kingdom, and we know that today may be the last opportunity for the soul to hear the Gospel.

The Joy and Blessing of Sharing Jesus Christ

There are wonderful blessings that evangelists enjoy. When you deliver tracts to hundreds of people in the evangelism field, you experience the joy that your heavenly Father gives you and the thrill of being used as a tool for the Gospel. When I focus on God's greatest concern, the salvation of souls, and follow Him with sincere obedience, I testify of the blessings that the Father abundantly provides even the things that I did not ask for. He grants the grace of becoming a person of faith that the world cannot give to the evangelist of Jesus Christ.

The reason why almighty God wants us to evangelize is to give us abundant blessings. First, He gives the reward of heaven to those who bring back souls that are more precious than the world to the Lord. In the work of saving souls, He wants to work with us. Second, He wants us to restore and sustain the thrill and assurance of salvation whenever we witness the Gospel. It is the wisdom of God prepared for us to live a life of powerfully proclaiming the cross of Jesus Christ.

Heavenly Father Sings for Me

On the way home today after witnessing the Gospel to hundreds of souls in the scorching heat of over 100 degrees Fahrenheit, my heavenly Father asked me, "Would you like to hear how much I love you?" and He sings a song.

> The Lord thy God in the midst of thee is mighty; he will save, he will rejoice over thee with joy; he will rest in his love, he will joy over thee with singing. (Zephaniah 3:17)

At that moment, the voice of the loving Father is heard from deep within. "You are the son I love, in whom I am well pleased." "That's right. Lord, I am the beloved son of God and the son with whom God is pleased. Until the day the Lord comes, I will live a life of witness that pleases You, my Father."

The Heavenly Father's Tears

The heavenly Father desires an intimate and loving fellowship with us humans. For us, who had no choice but to break and perish due to the fall of Adam and Eve, God gave the grace of redemption through the sacrifice and resurrection of His only-begotten Son, Jesus Christ on the cross. Even at this time, God is carrying out the work of forgiveness of sins and restoration of relationships through faithful servants of the Lord who obey and go and plant the seeds of the Gospel of salvation. The Lord looks at the countless perishing souls and weeps. He speaks with a sad heart to those who do not go outside to save their souls because they are passionate only about ministry and fellowship in the church while working with saints.

> Say not ye, There are yet four months, and then cometh harvest? behold, I say unto you, Lift up your eyes, and look on the fields; for they are white already to harvest. (John 4:35)

Our prayer should be, "Lord, send me many souls who are perishing."

GO! Evangelists play the role of light and salt in America.

The sad reality is that the United States, which played a pioneering role in world evangelization, is now falling into extreme secularism and materialism and is being reduced to a place where the Gospel must be accepted in reverse.

What we discover while doing on-the-road evangelism is that we only encounter saved saints in 2 to 3 percent of the cases. What's more, sadly, while evangelizing, you hardly ever see American or multiracial evangelists. God wants all of us saved saints to fulfill the role of light and salt in this spiritually dark land with the mission of holy priests.

We are a spiritual diaspora, living for a short time while fulfilling God's will in this world, longing for our eternal heavenly hometown. We are living in an era in which international migration and exchanges are rapidly increasing year by year amid a wave of globalization unprecedented in history. GO! Evangelists can be said to be the secret weapon of the Gospel that God has prepared for the completion of world missions.

People from all over the world, including Muslims, Hindus, and Buddhists, are living here in the United States, where persecution of Christians is increasing. For us evangelists who are living at the forefront of missions, a golden opportunity to spread the Gospel to multiracial groups is wide open.

Let's go out and proclaim for the final victory!

The paradigm of evangelism must change. As the world has become borderless, the rigid division between missions and evangelism has also become ineffective. Missionary work is important, but missionary work for immigrants in the United States is urgent, and when evangelizing them, you can embrace the souls of their motherland.

Now is the time for all of us GO! Evangelists to actively witness the Gospel to the countless multiracial souls. Whenever GO! Evangelist hears the voice of the Lord, saying, "Would you like to go with Me again to the place we went to last time, where many lost souls are still waiting for Me?" Today, I am running again with the Lord to the field of the Gospel.

The Essence of GO! Evangelism

GO evangelism is to go and declare the Gospel in obedience to the Lord's earnest call to go and proclaim. The core of GO! Evangelism is that evangelism is not done by our own abilities or methods, but by God. We GO! Evangelists simply obey and go, smile, and deliver the GO! tract with simple greetings and prayerful hearts. It is the faith that God creates that moves and saves the heart.

> And my speech and my preaching was not with enticing words of man's wisdom, but in demonstration of the Spirit and of power. (1 Corinthians 2:4)

> I have planted, Apollos watered; but God gave the increase. So then neither is he that planteth any thing, neither he that watereth; but God that giveth the increase. Now he that planteth and he that watereth are one: and every man shall receive his own reward according to his own labour. (1 Corinthians 3:6–8)

The Most Effective Method of GO! Evangelism

The most effective method of GO! Evangelism is to bear the heart of God the Father and go out whenever and wherever the opportunity gives, unconditionally, and deliver the GO! Evangelism tract, prepared as the core of the Gospel, to every soul you meet, sharing the seeds of the Gospel and blessing them in the name of Jesus Christ.

The easy yet powerful secret of GO! Evangelism lies in the GO! Evangelism Gospel tracts in more than 50 languages including children's illustrated versions. The following statements on the cover and initial pages of the GO! tract will instantly spark curiosity.

- Where will you spend eternity?

- How much time is left in your life?

- Are you saved?

- Where are you going now?

- Death comes suddenly and unexpectedly!

- If you aren't biblically saved at this moment, you are a heartbeat away from hell.

- You must prepare for your death today! Tomorrow may be too late!

The powerful seeds of the Gospel presents the content of accepting Jesus Christ as one's Lord and Savior through the core of the Gospel message, namely, the cross and resurrection, repentance and forgiveness, and the assurance of salvation through faith. It is believing and praying for what will be given.

GO! Evangelism enables the saints to live the life of an evangelist filled with the Holy Spirit, passionately and continuously through the work of going and proclaiming, with full dependence on the Holy Spirit.

Even now, when I think that there are countless perishing souls who will suffer eternal destruction if I do not go to the field and preach the Gospel, I pray to the Lord with a desperate heart for them and run out with GO! Gospel tracts.

And, behold, I come quickly; and my reward is with me, to give every man according as his work shall be. (Revelation 22:12)

GO! Evangelism Training Manual (The Greatest Joy of All!)

This evangelism manual is a textbook used for evangelism training in numerous churches over the past twenty years. Lectures are continued for four weeks, and in the fifth week, all the members who have completed four weeks of training are armed with one hundred GO! Gospel tracts each and sent out on the streets of downtown to experience the actual planting of the seeds of the Gospel.

The Purpose of Writing This Book

Through the details of the book you are reading now, the Holy Spirit will raise you all as passionate GO! Evangelists. This book will build and use you with much more powerful and faithful content than the four-week limited evangelism seminar. The real purpose of writing this book is to challenge and equip all of you to become bold GO! Evangelists by the inspiration of the Holy Spirit.

Many saints nationwide have been living the life of an evangelist for several years, and God's work of evangelizing by dozens to hundreds of people each and every week continues.

The purpose of this training manual is to establish a biblical view of salvation, to educate believers to believe accurately, to confess and testify of their faith, to possess the assurance of salvation based on the Word of God (not to an uncertain salvation based on experience and emotions), to glorify God through life, to illuminate this dark and sinful world with the Gospel of Jesus Christ, and to challenge and encourage all of us to live a life of witness like a flame.

> Jesus saith unto him, I am the way, the truth, and the life: no man cometh unto the Father, but by me. (John 14:6)

> Neither is there salvation in any other: for there is none other name under heaven given among men, whereby we must be saved. (Acts 4:12)

To be saved is to accept Jesus Christ as your Savior and Lord, to have all your sins forgiven, to be born again before God, to possess the kingdom of heaven, and to become a child of God.

What is most urgent for us believers living in this age is to restore and establish the joy of salvation and the thrill of salvation, through the assurance of salvation and experience of being born again, and to be transformed into a garden filled with the cool living water supplied by the Holy Spirit. On the rock of strong faith, we long for and prepare for the Day of Judgment to stand before the Lord, and we live the life of a mature and full-fledged believer that is pleasing to God.

Are you ready to meet the Lord?

Manual, Chapter 1.
The Assurance of Salvation and Being Born Again

I. What is salvation?

Salvation is the complete restoration of our relationship with God through Jesus Christ, from the child of wrath by nature and the sinner who had no choice but to be destroyed forever, to the child who can call God "Abba, Father" (see Ephesians 2:3; Romans 8:15; John 1:12).

When we are restored to a right relationship with God, which is the original purpose of creation, we will find the true meaning and purpose of life, enjoy true happiness and peace, and become a great seed for the glory of God and the channel of the Lord's intended blessings and Gospel.

You will be able to enjoy the abundant life God has bestowed upon you. Pastor John McArthur of Grace Community Church, a pioneer of the evangelical movement, defines salvation as follows: "Salvation involves forgiveness of sins through repentance and justification by faith, and is sealed by the process of regeneration through the Spirit." In other words, to receive the forgiveness of sins is salvation, and to be saved when you are born again is to be justified before God. Truly, we need this evangelical experience of salvation. We only live once. If you are not saved during your short life, you will never be given another chance.

Thou carriest them away as with a flood; they are as a sleep: in the morning they are like grass which groweth up. (Psalm 90:5)

II. What is the assurance of salvation?

The assurance of salvation is the basis of faith that believers must have and the first step for spiritual growth. "Assurance of salvation" means believing with certainty that I have been saved from sin and eternal death and become a child of God.

If you have a life of hopelessness, frustration, and insecurity in your heart, longing for the assurance of salvation and true joy, but still you still have no certainty; if you did not have faith to know whether you are going to heaven or hell when you die, how anxious would it be to live like this?

Believers must possess the assurance of salvation because God commands us to possess the assurance of salvation.

Examine yourselves, whether ye be in the faith; prove your own selves. Know ye not your own selves, how that Jesus Christ is in you, except ye be reprobates? (2 Corinthians 13:5)

He told us to test and confirm ourselves to see if we have the true faith for salvation, and to testify to it when it is confirmed that we have the true faith.

How can we prove our faith without the joy and excitement of the assurance of salvation?

The resurrected Lord rebukes the members of the Sardis Church, who believed that they were saved saints and lived an easy life, and He rebukes the members of the church living in the same weakness in this age.

> I know thy works, that thou hast a name that thou livest, and art dead. (Revelation 3:1)

"You are dead! Wake up!" When they look at the members of the church, they all look like they are alive and saved, but in reality they have not been saved (Revelation 3:4). They had the appearance of faith, but they did not know the power of the Gospel and the true meaning of salvation.

> When the Son of Man comes, shall he find faith on the earth? (Luke 18:8)

Even if you attend a good church, you may not be part of Christ. As faithful religious people, we fall into the danger of unimaginable shocks, surprises, terrifying fears, and despair on the last Day of Judgment while living like this every day with a vague expectation of going to heaven after death.

Warning against False Belief

> Not everyone that saith unto me, Lord, Lord, shall enter into the kingdom of heaven; but he that doeth the will of my Father which is in heaven. Many will say to me in that day, Lord, Lord, have we not prophesied in thy name? And in thy name have cast out devils? and in thy name done many wonderful works? And then will I profess unto them, I never knew you: depart from me, ye that work iniquity. (Matthew 7:21–23)

> The Son of man shall send forth his angels, and they shall gather out of his kingdom all things that offend,

and them which do iniquity; and shall cast them into a furnace of fire: there shall be wailing and gnashing of teeth. Then shall the righteous shine forth as the sun in the kingdom of their Father. Who hath ears to hear, let him hear. (Matthew 13:41–43)

III. Why do we need to be saved?

Unless you are saved, your soul will perish, and once you die, you will enter the terrible punishment of hell from which you cannot get out.

For all have sinned, and come short of the glory of God. (Romans 3:23)

There is none righteous, no, not one: there is none that understandeth, there is none that seeketh after God. They are all gone out of the way, they are together become unprofitable; there is none that doeth good, no, not one. (Romans 3:10–12)

For the wages of sin is death; but the gift of God is eternal life through Jesus Christ our Lord. (Romans 6:23)

And as it is appointed unto men once to die, but after this the judgment. (Hebrews 9:27)

Herein is our love made perfect, that we may have boldness in the day of judgment: because as he is, so are we in this world. (1 John 4:17)

IV. How can I be saved?

What we need to be saved is faith. The true faith to receive salvation is not your religious zeal, good deeds, efforts, or merits for salvation, but full faith and trust in what Jesus Christ accomplished perfectly on the cross.

When Jesus therefore had received the vinegar, he said, It is finished: and he bowed his head, and gave up the ghost. (John 19:30)

The most important thing that must precede the salvation of souls confirmed by faith and confession is to repent after realizing that you are a sinner who has no choice but to be destroyed before God.

Salvation in Faith through True Repentance

It is a miracle of God who worked on our souls to be saved through faith through true repentance. Only through repentance can we achieve salvation, become children of God, receive forgiveness of sins, and receive eternal life as a gift.

The essential event of the heart before fundamental repentance is to realize deeply that you are truly an ugly and wicked sinner before God, and to truly realize that you are a child of wrath without hope, a sinner destined to die forever. Without the naked realization and fundamental repentance of one's sinful heart and soul before God, true repentance is impossible.

Repent ye therefore, and be converted, that your sins may be blotted out, when the times of refreshing shall come from the presence of the Lord. (Acts 3:19)

What Is Repentance?

1. Confess and grieve for your sins before God.

> For I will declare mine iniquity; I will be sorry for my sin. (Psalm 38:18)

2. Have heartbreak before God for your sins.

> For godly sorrow worketh repentance to salvation not to be repented of: but the sorrow of the world worketh death. (2 Corinthians 7:10)

3. Repent of your sins before God and make a contrite confession.

> If we confess our sins, he is faithful and just to forgive us our sins, and to cleanse us from all unrighteousness. (1 John 1:9)

Why do we have to repent to be saved?

There is no forgiveness of sins without repentance, and there is no salvation without forgiveness of sins. An unrepentant and unforgiven person cannot enter the holy kingdom of God as an ugly soul where original sin and all the sins of life are still present.

1. We can receive forgiveness of sins through repentance and salvation through forgiveness of sins.

> Repent ye therefore, and be converted, that your sins may be blotted out, when the times of refreshing shall come from the presence of the Lord. (Acts 3:19)

2. We are saved through repentance and receive the Holy Spirit.

Then Peter said unto them, Repent, and be baptized every one of you in the name of Jesus Christ for the remission of sins, and ye shall receive the gift of the Holy Ghost. (Acts 2:38)

Those who confess Jesus Christ as their Lord and God receive the Holy Spirit as a gift, and through water of Baptism, the old man (that is, the sinful self) dies, and he becomes a new man publicly.

3. What is a truly repentant person who is pleasing to God?

If you have heard the Gospel and have been saved, the life of the saved must follow. If you have experienced true joy and emotion, you must have an active and passionate response to that grace, and a life of determination and obedience to live a holy and sanctified life pleasing to God must begin.

I beseech you therefore, brethren, by the mercies of God, that ye present your bodies a living sacrifice, holy, acceptable unto God, which is your reasonable service. (Romans 12:1)

Why should I confess Jesus as my Lord in front of the saints?

The believer's faith is confirmed by his confession of faith. First, believe with your heart, and then confess with your mouth. Faith comes from the heart, but the evidence of that faith is revealed by confession and declaration with the mouth.

That if thou shalt confess with thy mouth the Lord Jesus, and shalt believe in thine heart that God hath raised him from the dead, thou shalt be saved. For with the heart man believeth unto righteousness; and with the mouth confession is made unto salvation. (Romans 10:9–10)

Whosoever therefore shall confess me before men, him will I confess also before my Father which is in heaven. But whosoever shall deny me before men, him will I also deny before my Father which is in heaven. (Matthew 10:32–33)

Opening our mouths and confessing Jesus Christ as our Lord and Savior is very important for the salvation of souls. A confession that begins with a repentant heart must be confirmed by confession of the mouth. The confession of the mouth declares that Jesus Christ is Lord, Almighty God, Sovereign Ruler, King, Creator, and my eternal Savior.

We then, as workers together with him, beseech you also that ye receive not the grace of God in vain. (For he saith, I have heard thee in a time accepted, and in the day of salvation have I succoured thee: behold, now is the accepted time; behold, now is the day of salvation.) (2 Corinthians 6:1–2)

Behold, I stand at the door, and knock: if any man hear my voice, and open the door, I will come in to him, and will sup with him, and he with me. (Revelation 3:20)

You must be born again!

Jesus made it clear that unless a person is born again, he cannot see or enter the kingdom of God (John 3:3, 5, 7). The fundamental reason we need to be born again is that we are born of parents in the flesh without the Holy Spirit of God. Man is a fallen spirit just as Satan is a fallen spirit. A fallen spirit must be born again to become a new spirit. When we confess that Jesus is Lord and open our mouths to confess in front of people, the experience of being born again comes upon us. Confessing with our mouth what we believe in our heart plays an important role in the experience of being born again.

The Gospel of John clearly states the truth about being born again.

John said that being born again is of God (John 1:13) and of water and of the Spirit (John 3:5).

Jesus answered and said unto him, Verily, verily, I say unto thee, Except a man be born again, he cannot see the kingdom of God. (John 3:3)

Jesus answered, Verily, verily, I say unto thee, except a man be born of water and of the Spirit, he cannot enter into the kingdom of God. (John 3:5)

Marvel not that I said unto thee, Ye must be born again. (John 3:7)

Behold, the Lord's hand is not shortened, that it cannot save; neither his ear heavy, that it cannot hear: but your iniquities have separated between you and your God, and your sins have hid his face from you, that he will not hear. (Isaiah 59:1–2)

For our gospel came not unto you in word only, but also in power, and in the Holy Ghost, and in much assurance; as ye know what manner of men we were among you for your sake. (1 Thessalonians 1:5)

Which is come unto you, as it is in all the world; and bringeth forth fruit, as it doth also in you, since the day ye heard of it, and knew the grace of God in truth. (Colossians 1:6)

V. How can I know that I am truly saved?

The assurance and joy of salvation must be revealed through life changes and the fruits of the Holy Spirit. If you have the assurance of faith, you will always have a thirst for the Word of God. A close fellowship with God will begin, as well as a life of passion and obedience to please God.

1. I have a thirst for the Word of God.

Rooted and built up in him, and stablished in the faith, as ye have been taught, abounding therein with thanksgiving. (Colossians 2:7)

2. The Holy Spirit in me testifies.

The Spirit itself beareth witness with our spirit, that we are the children of God. (Romans 8:16)

3. My life is changed after receiving Jesus as my Lord and Savior.

The convincing evidence that we are truly saved by the grace of Jesus Christ is our genuinely changed appearance and lifestyle that proves that salvation.

Therefore if any man be in Christ, he is a new creature: old things are passed away; behold, all things are become new. (2 Corinthians 5:17)

4. I have love for brothers and sisters in Christ.

> We know that we have passed from death unto life, because we love the brethren. He that loveth not his brother abideth in death. (1 John 3:14)

5. I bear witness to God's compassion for lost souls.

> Say not ye, There are yet four months, and then cometh harvest? Behold, I say unto you, Lift up your eyes, and look on the fields; for they are white already to harvest. (John 4:35)

> Go ye into all the world, and preach the gospel to every creature. (Mark 16:15)

> For the Son of man is come to seek and to save that which was lost. (Luke 19:10)

> For this is good and acceptable in the sight of God our Saviour; who will have all men to be saved, and to come unto the knowledge of the truth. (1 Timothy 2:3–4)

> Then said Jesus to them again, Peace be unto you: as my Father hath sent me, even so send I you. (John 20:21)

VI. Pillars of Scripture that surely guarantee the salvation of our saints:

Who shall lay any thing to the charge of God's elect? It is God that justifieth. Who is he that condemneth? It is Christ that died, yea rather, that is risen again, who is even at the right hand of God, who also maketh intercession for us. (Romans 8:33–34)

For the which cause I also suffer these things: nevertheless I am not ashamed: for I know whom I have believed, and am persuaded that he is able to keep that which I have committed unto him against that day. (2 Timothy 1:12)

And I give unto them eternal life; and they shall never perish, neither shall any man pluck them out of my hand. (John 10:28)

When I have the faith that all my sins have been surely resolved and the conviction and thrill of what Christ has completely accomplished on the cross, and when I realize that there is nothing I can do to save myself now, I truly enjoy complete freedom from sin. From the beginning, those who make the decision to live for glory will enjoy the assurance and joy of true salvation.

For by one offering he hath perfected for ever them that are sanctified. (Hebrews 10:14)

For I will be merciful to their unrighteousness, and their sins and their iniquities will I remember no more. (Hebrews 8:12)

And their sins and iniquities will I remember no more. (Hebrews 10:17)

VII. The Three Aspects of God's Work of Salvation

God's work of salvation includes three aspects: past, present, and future.

1. Justification

Justification is how God declares sinners righteous before Him and thus eternally freed from the legal punishment for sin. This is the past aspect of salvation.

By justification, we are instantly saved from the penalty of sin (Romans chapters 1–4; Ephesians 2:1–10).

2. Sanctification: The life of Justified Believers

Sanctification, through which sinners are gradually liberated from sinful deeds by the power of the Holy Spirit, is the present aspect of salvation.

3. Glorification

Glorification, the future aspect of salvation, looks forward to the time when the saints will be completely freed from sin and brought into conformity with the image of Christ (Romans 8:18–30; 2 Timothy 4:1–18).

Manual, Chapter 2:
The Great Blessings of the GO! Evangelists

If you are a believer who has truly received salvation after hearing the Gospel of Jesus Christ, the life of the saved must follow. That we are saved is a gift of God's grace that cannot be received without emotion. If you are a believer who has experienced such joy and emotion, shouldn't you be living a life that is a response to that grace?

From now on, that natural response must be expressed in obedience to live as a saved saint for the glory of God and the channel of blessing and the Gospel with which God is very pleased. The salvation that God wants is a salvation of the whole person, in which the soul and body are saved together.

> But if the Spirit of him that raised up Jesus from the dead dwell in you, he that raised up Christ from the dead shall also quicken your mortal bodies by his Spirit that dwelleth in you. (Romans 8:11)

When the saints experience being born again, the inner man has been regenerated, but because our fragile body has not been replaced with a new one, the instinct and sinful nature that are still living in the body are changed into holiness, and we strive to become a temple in which the Holy Spirit of God dwells.

> I beseech you therefore, brethren, by the mercies of God, that ye present your bodies a living sacrifice,

holy, acceptable unto God, which is your reasonable service. And be not conformed to this world: but be ye transformed by the renewing of your mind, that ye may prove what is that good, and acceptable, and perfect, will of God. (Romans 12:1–2)

If we are saved and become the Lord's, all areas of our lives must become a life of sacrifice that God is very pleased with.

The Bible stresses that all must stand before the judgment seat of Christ.

And as it is appointed unto men once to die, but after this the judgment. (Hebrews 9:27)

The Bible speaks of two judgments.

Verily, verily, I say unto you, He that heareth my word, and believeth on him that sent me, hath everlasting life, and shall not come into condemnation; but is passed from death unto life. (John 5:24)

For we must all appear before the judgment seat of Christ; that every one may receive the things done in his body, according to that he hath done, whether it be good or bad. Knowing therefore the terror of the Lord, we persuade men; but we are made manifest unto God; and I trust also are made manifest in your consciences. (2 Corinthians 5:10–11)

Are you really ready?

The wise saints are those who long for the eternal kingdom of heaven and prepare for the day when they will stand before the Lord. They are true believers who live a holy and sanctified life, knowing that their eternal destiny is determined by how they live on this earth and that all thoughts and actions of the present moment are being recorded. They live with a clear sense of calling.

We shall all stand before the judgment seat of Christ. . . . So then every one of us shall give account of himself to God. (Romans 14:10, 12)

Herein is our love made perfect, that we may have boldness in the day of judgment: because as he is, so are we in this world. (1 John 4:17)

Wherefore the rather, brethren, give diligence to make your calling and election sure: for if ye do these things, ye shall never fall: for so an entrance shall be ministered unto you abundantly into the everlasting kingdom of our Lord and Saviour Jesus Christ. (2 Peter 1:10–11)

1. We must become like Jesus Christ.

Wherefore, my beloved, as ye have always obeyed, not as in my presence only, but now much more in my absence, work out your own salvation with fear and trembling. (Philippians 2:12)

Being filled with the fruits of righteousness, which are by Jesus Christ, unto the glory and praise of God. (Philippians 1:11)

At that time, Paul, who was writing the Book of Philippians while in prison, was in a situation in which he could never be happy. Nevertheless, the reason why we exhort free people out of prison to rejoice is that our saints who have heavenly citizenship have different reasons for joy, different values, and different views of happiness from those of this world.

For us citizens of heaven, the future is more important than the present, and the judgment of the Lord in front of the judgment seat of Bema, the Kingdom of God, which is coming soon, is much more important than the evaluation of people in this world, and our eternity is decided.

He says that we must all stand before the judgment seat of Christ and be judged according to what we have done on this earth. If you are a saint who longs for and waits for the day to stand before the Lord, you must become like Jesus Christ through your daily life.

> Therefore if any man be in Christ, he is a new creature: old things are passed away; behold, all things are become new. (2 Corinthians 5:17)

> And he said to them all, If any man will come after me, let him deny himself, and take up his cross daily, and follow me. (Luke 9:23)

> Even so faith, if it hath not works, is dead, being alone. (James 2:17)

> And why call ye me, Lord, Lord, and do not the things which I say? (Luke 6:46)

> 2. We must live the life of a witness that is pleasing to God.

The joy and thrill of the assurance of salvation must be accompanied by a longing heart for lost souls. If there is an emotion of being saved, the emotion of being sent must follow.

If I, a believer who has the joy and emotion of being saved and becoming a child of God, am indifferent to the salvation of countless other perishing souls around me, then God, who gave even the life of His only-begotten Son, Jesus Christ, to save me, cannot be pleased.

The saints must have pain that is constantly grieving for the countless unsaved souls. If you are a saved believer, you must realize that God most anxiously waits for you to testify the Gospel to dying souls and live the life of a witness. That is the heart of our heavenly Father.

> I say the truth in Christ, I lie not, my conscience also bearing me witness in the Holy Ghost, that I have great heaviness and continual sorrow in my heart. (Romans 9:1–2)

> And this is the Father's will which hath sent me, that of all which he hath given me I should lose nothing, but should raise it up again at the last day. (John 6:39)

What our heavenly Father is most pleased with is evangelism that saves perishing souls, who are more precious than the world. It is the greatest privilege and happiness in life to be used as an evangelist who spreads the Gospel of salvation of Jesus Christ through my life.

Abundant Blessings Granted to GO! Evangelists

If we are called as evangelists who save souls who are more precious than the world, this calling is an honor through God's grace. Just thinking about whether God has chosen me, saved me, recognized me as an ambassador of the kingdom of heaven, given me a glorious mission, and allowed me to live as a witness to save lost souls fills me with gratitude, joy, emotion, and praise.

1. You will experience the joy and thrill of working with the Holy Spirit.

> But ye shall receive power, after that the Holy Ghost is come upon you: and ye shall be witnesses unto me both in Jerusalem, and in all Judaea, and in Samaria, and unto the uttermost part of the earth. (Acts 1:8)

> And my speech and my preaching was not with enticing words of man's wisdom, but in demonstration of the Spirit and of power. (1 Corinthians 2:4)

2. You will grow rapidly as a mature and passionate believer.

> But none of these things move me, neither count I my life dear unto myself, so that I might finish my course with joy, and the ministry, which I have received of the Lord Jesus, to testify the gospel of the grace of God. (Acts 20:24)

3. He raises us up as worshipers overflowing with gratitude and emotion.

He moves us to be greatly used in God's work of salvation, and He makes us happy worshipers overflowing with thanks and praise.

Make a joyful noise unto the Lord, all ye lands. Serve the Lord with gladness: come before his presence with singing. Know ye that the Lord he is God: it is he that hath made us, and not we ourselves; we are his people, and the sheep of his pasture. Enter into his gates with thanksgiving, and into his courts with praise: be thankful unto him, and bless his name. For the Lord is good; his mercy is everlasting; and his truth endureth to all generations. (Psalm 100:1–5)

4. As we long for the great reward of heaven, He makes us run.

And, behold, I come quickly; and my reward is with me, to give every man according as his work shall be. (Revelation 22:12)

And they that be wise shall shine as the brightness of the firmament; and they that turn many to righteousness as the stars for ever and ever. (Daniel 12:3)

5. He grants the blessing of intimate fellowship and walking with God.

To the saints who deeply understand and obey the mystery in Jesus Christ, and who live the life of an evangelist with a heart for the lost souls of our heavenly Father, God bestows the true freedom, peace, satisfaction, joy of life, and leisure of life that the world cannot afford.

The Lord thy God in the midst of thee is mighty; he will save, he will rejoice over thee with joy; he will rest in his love, he will joy over thee with singing. (Zephaniah 3:17)

GO! Evangelism Doctrinal Statement

GO! Evangelism Ministry believes the following doctrinal points:

The Bible is the infallible Word of God. It is His holy and inspired Word, and it is of supreme and final authority.

We believe in one God, eternally existing in three persons: Father, Son, and Holy Spirit.

Jesus Christ was conceived by the Holy Spirit and born of the Virgin Mary. He led a sinless life, took on Himself all our sins, died, and rose again. He is seated at the right hand of the Father as our mediator and advocate.

All men everywhere are lost and face the judgment of God, and they need to come to a saving knowledge of Jesus Christ through His shed blood on the cross.

Christ is coming back soon for His Church.

And, behold, I come quickly; and my reward is with me, to give every man according as his work shall be. (Revelation 22:12)

Chapter 6: GO! Evangelism: So Simple, Yet So Powerful

Are you obeying and doing what the Lord commanded you to do?

Go ye into all the world, and preach the gospel to every creature. (Mark 16:15)

Jesus gave this command to His disciples in what is known as the "Great Commission." It was Jesus' last command to His disciples after His resurrection and prior to His ascension back to heaven.

Jesus' command was not an option or a suggestion. It was a mandate to proclaim the Gospel. *Mandate* is defined as "authorization, command, decree, directive, injunction, instruction, and sanction."

God's command to go everywhere and tell everyone appears in all four Gospels and the Book of Acts, as seen below:

Go ye therefore, and teach all nations, baptizing them in the name of the Father, and of the Son, and of the Holy Ghost: teaching them to observe all things whatsoever I have commanded you: and, lo, I am with you alway, even unto the end of the world. Amen. (Matthew 28:19–20)

And he said unto them, Go ye into all the world, and preach the gospel to every creature. (Mark 16:15)

And said unto them, Thus it is written, and thus it behoved Christ to suffer, and to rise from the dead the third day: and that repentance and remission of sins should be preached in his name among all nations, beginning at Jerusalem. And ye are witnesses of these things. (Luke 24:46–48)

Then said Jesus to them again, Peace be unto you: as my Father hath sent me, even so send I you. (John 20:21)

But ye shall receive power, after that the Holy Ghost is come upon you: and ye shall be witnesses unto me both in Jerusalem, and in all Judaea, and in Samaria, and unto the uttermost part of the earth. (Acts 1:8)

The Great Commission in Mark's Gospel seems to indicate something of its significance. Mark's Gospel has just sixteen chapters and is the shortest of the Gospels, and yet the Great Commission appeared to be the top priority.

Prior to His command, Jesus spoke these words to them. "All power is given unto me in heaven and in earth" (Matthew 28:18). Therefore, Jesus has the right to make this command to all of us. All of us who claim to have been born again, are washed in the blood of the Lamb, are saved from sin, have heard the Gospel message, and have responded are responsible for proclaiming this same Good News, called the Gospel of Jesus Christ, to all perishing souls. This is a mandate commanded to every born-again Christian.

God is urging us to recapture our evangelistic and missionary zeal.

We should remember the prayer of our Founding Father Robert Hunt, upon landing at Jamestown in 1607:

> We do hereby dedicate this land, and ourselves, to reach the people within the shores with the gospel of Jesus Christ, and to raise up godly generations after us, and with these generations take the kingdom of God to all the earth.

It's time to proclaim the Gospel simply and powerfully to as many people as possible, as too many souls are perishing without knowing Jesus Christ. If anyone die without Jesus Christ, it will be the worst mistake, as the person will be on the way to hell. Don't let anyone convince you that when you die it will be all over!

> And as it is appointed unto men once to die, but after this the judgment (Hebrews 9:27)

> And whosoever was not found written in the book of life was cast into the lake of fire. (Revelation 20:15)

The simplest and yet most powerful evangelism method is to follow the instructions given by the Lord in the following three Scripture passages:

> I have planted, Apollos watered; but God gave the increase. So then neither is he that planteth any thing, neither he that watereth; but God that giveth the increase. Now he that planteth and he that watereth

are one: and every man shall receive his own reward according to his own labour. (1 Corinthians 3:6–8)

And my speech and my preaching was not with enticing words of man's wisdom, but in demonstration of the Spirit and of power: that your faith should not stand in the wisdom of men, but in the power of God. (1 Corinthians 2:4–5)

For though I preach the gospel, I have nothing to glory of: for necessity is laid upon me; yea, woe is unto me, if I preach not the gospel! (1 Corinthians 9:16)

We GO! Evangelists should be filled with and empowered by the Holy Spirit.

As clearly stated above, the most crucial and important thing all GO! Evangelists should know is to be filled with, empowered by, and guided by the Holy Spirit. You cannot proclaim the good news about Jesus in your own strength. God does not intend you to.

The most effective evangelism is taking the initiative in the power of the Holy Spirit and leaving the results to God, who gives the increase. The final results do not depend on how well we share the Gospel with enticing words of man's wisdom. We should leave the results in demonstration of the Spirit and of power.

In order to stay as an effective and powerful GO! Evangelist and maintain a deep burden for souls, we should pay less attention to what we do for the Lord, as the focus is on everything He does through us, and this always requires a totally surrendered heart filled with the Holy Spirit.

We will go out and plant the powerful seeds of the Gospel with a sincere and pleasant smile, handing out tracts and saying, "Hi, I would like to share good news with you," or simply, "Hi, I have good news for you!" If they ask, "What is it about?" then tell them the truth: "It is a Gospel tract. It will show you how to get to heaven." We have many GO! Evangelists handing out several hundred GO! Gospel tracts each week, diligently planting seeds of the Gospel, knowing that the Holy Spirit is working to save these perishing souls of all ethnic groups.

God has given us a mission to plant and water seeds of the Gospel. However, neither Paul nor Apollos was able to cause that seed to grow. It is only God who gives the growth. And yet nothing can grow without a seed first being planted.

The best ways to strengthen our passion as GO! Evangelists are to read His Word daily and to pray continually for the salvation of these people we meet on a daily basis. When our hearts and minds are filled with Christ, we simply can't help but to maintain a passion for sharing Him with many others. The most blazing evangelists are those who have a burning heart that is on fire for Christ.

If you simply refuse to proclaim the Gospel to those you claim to care about, those you encounter on a daily basis, and if they die without knowing Jesus Christ, their blood stains will be on your hands, as God warned all of us.

> When I say unto the wicked, Thou shalt surely die; and
> thou givest him not warning, nor speakest to warn the

wicked from his wicked way, to save his life; the same
wicked man shall die in his iniquity; but his blood will
I require at thine hand. (Ezekiel 3:18)

If God has given us the command to go and proclaim the Gospel, why is it that we struggle with evangelism?

For one thing, most Christian do not consider themselves as
evangelists, and they certainly do not feel it is their responsibility
to proclaim the Gospel. Yes, they are right in one sense; most
people are not evangelists. However, Jesus commanded all of us
to proclaim the Gospel.

For though I preach the gospel, I have nothing to glory
of: for necessity is laid upon me; yea, woe is unto me, if
I preach not the gospel! For if I do this thing willingly,
I have a reward: but if against my will, a dispensation
of the gospel is committed unto me. (1 Corinthians
9:16–17)

So Simple, Yet So Powerful!

This is where GO! Evangelism comes in. In order for all
of us to become energetic and enthusiastic evangelists, God
provided us with powerful seeds of the Gospel, GO! Evangelism
Gospel tracts, with twelve to twenty-four colorful pages each,
armed with about 1,300 words, in over fifty languages.

Although not too many Christians are articulate, fluent,
silver-tongued, and well-spoken, all of us can smile and pass out
GO! Gospel tracts, biblically solid and with a powerful Gospel
message, with a sincere and pleasant smile. We can say, "Hi, I

would like to share good news with you." If they ask, "What is it about?" tell them the truth with an even more joyous and gracious smile: "It is a Gospel tract. It will show you how to get to heaven. I hope to see you in heaven soon."

This way, you will be doing exactly what the Lord commanded you to do.

Go ye into all the world, and preach the gospel to every creature. (Mark 16:15)

The Gospel is meant for all the *ethnos*—for all the various races and colors, all the cultures of the world, all the civilizations that now exist worldwide. The mixture of nations has changed so dramatically in the past several decades. Drive down the street to a different neighborhood, and you'll soon find a culture very different from your own.

God has bestowed a special blessing upon us in these last days. As a Christian living in the United States, we are now abundantly blessed to have opportunities to plant powerful seeds of the Gospel to every creature. There are people from all over the world now living in the U.S., and they all understand simple conversation such as, "Hi, how are you? Good morning, I have good news for you. Jesus loves you."

Rather than purposely staying away from someone from other cultures, you need to be brave enough to go to them with GO! Gospel tracts of the appropriate language and start passing out the salvation message. The seeds of the Gospel that you plant will grow and bear fruit by God.

For if I do this thing willingly, I have a reward: but
if against my will, a dispensation of the gospel is
committed unto me. (1 Corinthians 9:17)

What does all this mean for you, GO! Evangelist?

It doesn't mean you have to buy a ticket and fly to the other
side of the world to proclaim the Gospel. He expects you to take
the Gospel to everyone you meet on the streets, everyone in the
different ethnic groups, cultures, and civilizations that are in
your neighborhood. In fact, your mission field is right down
your street or on the other side of your city in a neighborhood
where the cultures are different than your own.

Open your eyes and look around you! Jesus told the
disciples that the fields were "white already to harvest" (John
4:35). If you look around your neighborhood, you will also
find that the fields around you are white unto harvest as well.
All these perishing people are waiting for someone to come to
them with the salvation message of Jesus Christ, and you are the
evangelist God wants to send them. These perishing people will
accept the powerful seeds of the Gospel as the Holy Spirit will
open their hearts.

Romans 10:14 clearly states:

How then shall they call on him in whom they have not
believed? and how shall they believe in him of whom
they have not heard? and how shall they hear without
a preacher?

The Bible clearly speaks to all people and all cultures
that Jesus Christ is the only faithful example of divine love in

interpersonal relationships and communication. Jesus is God with us—the reality of the love of God in human experience.

What kind of persons should we GO! Evangelists become when we meet all the various races and colors? We can find some direct instructions in Scripture.

Let this mind be in you, which was also in Christ Jesus. (Philippians 2:5)

For even hereunto were ye called: because Christ also suffered for us, leaving us an example, that ye should follow his steps. (1 Peter 2:21)

Jesus sends us out through the Great Commission into all the world. As His messengers, we are to follow closely His example in union with Him.

God's Word is meant to be shared with everyone. God promises us that when we obey and share the Gospel, His Spirit will do the rest. We can rest in knowing that God's Word will not return empty, but it will accomplish what God pleases.

So shall my word be that goeth forth out of my mouth: it shall not return unto me void, but it shall accomplish that which I please, and it shall prosper in the thing whereto I sent it. (Isaiah 55:11)

God reveals the secret to GO! Evangelists.

It is not our eloquent and enticing speech that moves the heart of an unbeliever. It is not of man's wisdom but is in the power of the Holy Spirit.

And my speech and my preaching was not with enticing words of man's wisdom, but in demonstration of the Spirit and of power. (1 Corinthians 2:4)

If you decide to go out to the streets today, God will give you an opportunity to proclaim to any area of more than 332 million people in the U.S., including those from foreign countries. Your opportunity is wide open. Make sure to visit our ministry websites below and decide which language version and the quantity of your selected version. Your order will be shipped within two to three days to your location.

www.GospelTracts.org

www.BibleTracts.org

How can born again Christians today effectively and powerfully carry out the Great Commission? Well, it certainly includes actually going out to the streets in your town to plant the seeds of the Gospel in everyone you meet with a pleasant greeting.

Most of the things that take up our time and energy now won't matter much in a million years. What really will matter is whether people are with their God, the Creator, or if they will be separated forever from Him in everlasting burning hell. Therefore, whether we obey and carry out the Great Commission today will matter for all of eternity.

In this day and age, it is very sad to witness the Gospel through the personal evangelism or relational evangelism we have been doing. That is, there are simply too many souls who need to be saved, especially when the Second Coming of our Lord is imminent. We simply do not have enough time. We must share the seeds of the Gospel to as many lost souls as possible without any delays and hesitations.

In evangelism, while planting the seeds of the Gospel, God is fully responsible for the salvation of each soul. We plant seeds in all the souls we meet while praying for the salvation of that soul. The following Bible passages clearly explain why evangelism by planting the seeds of the Gospel prepared by the Lord can witness the Gospel to far more souls.

> And my speech and my preaching was not with enticing words of man's wisdom, but in demonstration of the Spirit and of power: that your faith should not stand in the wisdom of men, but in the power of God. (1 Corinthians 2:4–5)

> I have planted, Apollos watered; but God gave the increase. So then neither is he that planteth any thing, neither he that watereth; but God that giveth the increase. Now he that planteth and he that watereth are one: and every man shall receive his own reward according to his own labour. (1 Corinthians 3:6–8)

Please remember, it is our God that gives the increase. It's so simple, yet so powerful, as we totally rely upon God's saving sovereignty!

> And, behold, I come quickly; and my reward is with me, to give every man according as his work shall be. (Revelation 22:12)

Chapter 7: Have You Received the Holy Spirit? Then GO Now!

There is nothing peaceful and stable about waiting in the presence of God, because at any moment the quiet solitude of prayer and meditation on His glory can easily explode into a volcanic eruption of praise and thanksgiving, as the reality of who He really is hits us like a high-voltage power cable and explosion at any moment.

In chapter 2 of Acts, a group of 120 believers were waiting. They weren't quite sure what to do, as Jesus had just said to wait for the gift of the Holy Spirit. They didn't know what to expect, because none of them had ever seen the Holy Spirit. Therefore, in the midst of their waiting, praying, and meditating on the holiness and goodness that was demonstrated in the life of Jesus, they were hit by a power much stronger than the entire universe. Their quiet meditation turned into a high-voltage explosion that turned the world upside down.

God is urgently calling His sons and daughters to experience living in the realm of His spirit. Like the 120 in the upper room, we can't really comprehend exactly what the final outcome of our seeking and waiting will be.

In the second chapter of the Book of Acts, we read about the beginning of the church. The first chapter tells us of Jesus meeting with the apostles on the Mount of Olives and telling them that they are to be His witnesses to all the world. He also tells them that they are to wait in Jerusalem until they receive power from on high. Then He ascends out of their sight. So they go to Jerusalem to wait and pray.

And when the day of Pentecost was fully come, they were all with one accord in one place. And suddenly there came a sound from heaven as of a rushing mighty wind, and it filled all the house where they were sitting. And there appeared unto them cloven tongues like as of fire, and it sat upon each of them. And they were all filled with the Holy Ghost, and began to speak with other tongues, as the Spirit gave them utterance.

And there were dwelling at Jerusalem Jews, devout men, out of every nation under heaven. Now when this was noised abroad, the multitude came together, and were confounded, because that every man heard them speak in his own language. And they were all amazed and marvelled, saying one to another, Behold, are not all these which speak Galilaeans? And how hear we every man in our own tongue, wherein we were born? Parthians, and Medes, and Elamites, and the dwellers in Mesopotamia, and in Judaea, and Cappadocia, in Pontus, and Asia, Phrygia, and Pamphylia, in Egypt, and in the parts of Libya about Cyrene, and strangers of Rome, Jews and proselytes, Cretes and Arabians, we do hear them speak in our tongues the wonderful works of God. And they were all amazed, and were in doubt, saying one to another, What meaneth this? Others mocking said, These men are full of new wine.

But Peter, standing up with the eleven, lifted up his voice, and said unto them, Ye men of Judaea, and all ye that dwell at Jerusalem, be this known unto you, and hearken to my words: for these are not drunken, as ye suppose, seeing it is but the third hour of the day. But this is that which was spoken by the prophet Joel. (Acts 2:1–16)

Therefore let all the house of Israel know assuredly, that God hath made that same Jesus, whom ye have crucified, both Lord and Christ.

Now when they heard this, they were pricked in their heart, and said unto Peter and to the rest of the apostles, Men and brethren, what shall we do? Then Peter said unto them, Repent, and be baptized every one of you in the name of Jesus Christ for the remission of sins, and ye shall receive the gift of the Holy Ghost. For the promise is unto you, and to your children, and to all that are afar off, even as many as the Lord our God shall call. And with many other words did he testify and exhort, saying, Save yourselves from this untoward generation. (Acts 2:36–41)

"Brethren, What Shall We Do?"

During St. Peter's strong and powerful sermon to the Jews gathered for the Pentecost festival, in which he told them that God raised up Jesus, who was crucified at the instigation of the Jerusalem Jewish leaders, and made Him "both Lord and Christ," Peter's hearers were "pricked in their heart" and were moved to ask what they could do to turn their lives around.

Peter's powerful words bit deep into their hearts until the guilt was too much to bear and they cried out loud, "What shall we do?"

All of them knew that they were guilty, that they had crucified Jesus Christ, the Son of God, with their sins. But now they had repented of their sins, as demonstrated in the following passage.

"Ye shall receive the gift of the Holy Ghost."

Then Peter said unto them, Repent, and be baptized every one of you in the name of Jesus Christ for the remission of sins, and ye shall receive the gift of the Holy Ghost. (Acts 2:38)

Peter exhorted the crowd, "Repent . . . and ye shall receive the gift of the Holy Ghost." He warned them and pleaded with them, "Save yourselves from this corrupt generation."

Not everyone heeded this urgent call. But about three thousand people did! Not everyone will listen to our Gospel message. But some will, if we do the job God has called us to do!

In order to do that, however, we GO! Evangelists need to have the Holy Spirit living within us. That happens only when we accept Jesus Christ into our lives as our Lord and Savior. There is absolutely no other way in which we can receive the gift of the Holy Spirit. It is at that moment that we are baptized with the Holy Spirit, and it is something that can only happen once. There are occasions, though, in which we need to be filled by the Holy Spirit to fulfil a specific mission that God has called us to do. We have to have the Holy Spirit living within us if we desire Him to fill us.

All Believers Must Receive the Gift of the Holy Spirit

The core of the new covenant promised to us by the Lord who completed the work of complete redemption is that He will send the Holy Spirit. The Holy Spirit is a Person of the living God, not a power or influence we can use. The Bible reveals to us that God is three Persons: the Father, the Son, and the Holy Spirit. The Holy Spirit is God over us and within us.

When the Holy Spirit came upon us, He regenerated us and sanctified us. He boldly plants the seeds of the Gospel in countless lost souls. All the lives of the saints and the subject of all our visions have changed to the Lord.

Steps to Receive the Gift of the Holy Spirit

1. You must first repent.

You must first recognize your sins. You must admit to yourself that you have sinned. You must feel sorrow for your sins. You must forsake your sins. You must confess your sins. You must make restitution.

2. You must believe the Gospel.

Your faith must be based on the promises of Jesus. Jesus says, "If anyone is thirsty and wants to be filled with the Holy Spirit, first come to Me and drink." That is, you must thoroughly believe in the Gospel of Jesus Christ and come out. We must first hear and realize the Gospel of the cross.

In the last day, that great day of the feast, Jesus stood and cried, saying, If any man thirst, let him come unto me, and drink. He that believeth on me, as the scripture hath said, out of his belly shall flow rivers of living water. (John 7:37–38)

3. You must be baptized.

Baptism is significant in that it represents the forgiveness and cleansing from sin that comes through faith in Jesus Christ. Baptism publicly acknowledges one's true confession of faith and belief in the Gospel message.

Does Acts 2:38 teach that one must be baptized to be saved?

Regarding baptism and salvation, the Bible clearly teaches that salvation is by grace through faith in Jesus Christ and not through any other ordinance, including baptism.

Therefore, it would be a mistake to claim that baptism, or any other act, is a necessary procedure for salvation. So why do some people conclude that we must be baptized to be saved? Here I want to share with you the clear answer the Holy Spirit gives me.

Please read Acts 2:38 slowly and carefully again:

Then Peter said unto them, Repent, and be baptized every one of you in the name of Jesus Christ for the remission of sins, and ye shall receive the gift of the Holy Ghost. (Acts 2:38)

Here, the true meaning of *baptism* is not "a certain ritual to receive baptism," but the spiritual meaning of true baptism must be realized.

The True Meaning of Baptism

Baptism is a symbol of conversion in the Bible. Baptism means dying to our sinful past and resurrecting to experience a new life of joy and victory in Jesus Christ. Baptism is done for the sake of one's own happiness and joy to bury the previous life of disobedience to God and to live a new life in Christ.

1. How important is baptism?

Salvation is obtained through faith in Jesus Christ, but it is expressed through baptism. Jesus made it clear that being baptized is essential in the Christian life.

2. How was Jesus baptized?

Jesus went into the Jordan River and came up from the water. Jesus was baptized by immersion in water.

And it came to pass in those days, that Jesus came from Nazareth of Galilee, and was baptized of John in Jordan. And straightway coming up out of the water, he saw the heavens opened, and the Spirit like a dove descending upon him. (Mark 1:9–10)

3. What does water symbolize?

Water symbolizes spiritual purity. It also symbolizes purity and new beginnings. Everyone must begin a new life through baptism.

And now why tarriest thou? arise, and be baptized, and wash away thy sins, calling on the name of the Lord. (Acts 22:16)

> Jesus answered, Verily, verily, I say unto thee, Except a
> man be born of water and of the Spirit, he cannot enter
> into the kingdom of God. (John 3:5)

> For as many of you as have been baptized into Christ
> have put on Christ. (Galatians 3:27)

4. What is the symbolic meaning of the baptismal service?

Baptism symbolizes washing away from a previous sinful life and starting a new life in Jesus Christ. Baptism is also a sign of the experience of Christ's death, burial, and resurrection through the death of the sinful self and the birth of a new life.

Just as Jesus died and was buried and resurrected, the new Christian is baptized to die to his previous sinful life, and after being buried in water, he is resurrected to a new life endowed with the power of the Holy Spirit.

The person being baptized first puts down his sinful life, immerses himself in the water, and then comes up to live a new life in Jesus.

> Therefore we are buried with him by baptism into
> death: that like as Christ was raised up from the dead
> by the glory of the Father, even so we also should walk
> in newness of life. (Romans 6:4)

5. What is the most important thing that accompanies baptism in water?

True baptism in water is accompanied by the baptism of the Holy Spirit. To be baptized with the Holy Spirit means to be completely immersed in the Holy Spirit, which means that the Holy Spirit comes into your life and completely transforms your life.

Jesus answered, Verily, verily, I say unto thee, Except a man be born of water and of the Spirit, he cannot enter into the kingdom of God. (John 3:5)

The true meaning of baptism is that we have been saved because Jesus died on the cross and rose from the dead. In baptism, we die with the Lord and resurrect with the Lord.

Even now, the baptismal rite in Baptist churches is the true meaning of the baptismal rite, so that when our entire body is immersed in the water, we are buried with Christ, and when we are taken out of the water, we are resurrected with the risen Lord.

Buried with him in baptism, wherein also ye are risen with him through the faith of the operation of God, who hath raised him from the dead. (Colossians 2:12)

The meaning of true baptism is a sign of a good conscience toward God. Baptism is the mark of a person who is saved, and it is a testimony to obey the Word of God with a good conscience. It is wrong to think that it is a ceremony to wash away sins or that salvation is achieved only through Baptism.

You must have remission of sins. In order to be cleansed from sins, you must exercise faith in Jesus Christ unto repentance. As you sincerely repent, you can receive a remission of sins, which brings joy and peace of conscience to your soul.

You will receive the gift of the Holy Spirit. The gift of the Holy Spirit is bestowed on all who have covenanted with Jesus Christ in baptism.

Now, If You Have Received the Gift of the Holy Spirit, Then GO!

But ye shall receive power, after that the Holy Ghost is come upon you: and ye shall be witnesses unto me both in Jerusalem, and in all Judaea, and in Samaria, and unto the uttermost part of the earth. (Acts 1:8)

There are countless perishing souls in total darkness in your very own neighborhood, just outside of your four walls, who have absolutely no idea how much they need Jesus Christ in their lives, let alone the countless billions around the world. But to think worldwide, we first need to think local.

In order to reach the world with the Gospel, we must first begin in our own backyard and our immediate neighborhoods, where you can go out and start distributing GO! Gospel tracts in over fifty languages.

Special Power Is Essential for GO! Evangelists

Please read these passages thoroughly from Luke and Acts below:

And, behold, I send the promise of my Father upon you: but tarry ye in the city of Jerusalem, until ye be endued with power from on high. (Luke 24:49)

But ye shall receive power, after that the Holy Ghost is come upon you: and ye shall be witnesses unto me both in Jerusalem, and in all Judaea, and in Samaria, and unto the uttermost parts of the earth. (Acts 1:8)

In Acts 1:8, Jesus says that power must come first. In both of these texts, Jesus is sending the believers from Jerusalem until all the nations are evangelized.

Jesus is not suggesting here an occasional word of witness in our same circle of culture. He is talking about ever-expanding efforts to penetrate more and more of Satan's strongholds of unbelief. This is why special power is essential for an expanding witness to Christ.

Acts 1:8 emphasizes two important things we need to know:

1. The Holy Spirit empowers GO! Evangelists.

2. Spirit-filled GO! Evangelists witness about Jesus to all creatures.

Our greatest need today is for the power of the Holy Spirit, in order that we might reach every creature living in all the world.

Are you still hesitating and reluctant to go out? "I stammer; I'm too shy to witness; I don't know enough Bible verses; I have face-to-face phobia; I have fear of rejection."

This is why God has given us GO! Evangelism tracts, the powerful seeds of the Gospel in over fifty languages. Your excuses above don't apply to GO! Evangelism. Why? Because all you have to do is pray for those perishing souls you will meet and equip yourself with GO! tracts of your choice before you go out by visiting our ministry sites:

www.GospelTracts.org

www.BibleTracts.org

You will be holding in your hand GO! Gospel tracts, biblically solid and with the powerful life-Saving Gospel message—a great witnessing tool. These Gospel tracts have the powerful message to save many perishing souls of all ethnic groups.

You simply hand out GO! tracts, the seeds of eternal life, with a sincere and pleasant smile, and say "Hi, I would like to share good news with you." Or you can simply say, "Hi, I have good news for you!" If they ask, "What is it about?" then tell them the truth. "It is a Gospel tract. It will show you how to get to heaven."

Winning souls is fulfilling the Great Commission! It is Jesus' command to all His followers or disciples to spread His teachings to all the nations of the world. It is a personal instruction from Jesus Christ and a special calling to His disciples. Jesus calls every Christian to step out in faith and spread the good news.

Many souls who don't know Jesus are dying every day and going to hell, according to the Word of God! Souls are lost in sin forever! Souls without Jesus are perishing! This is why we Christians must get busy in spreading the Gospel to all perishing souls, using this powerful Gospel tool.

Please remember two Bible passages below that will tell you why we GO! Evangelists should focus on planting the seeds of the Gospel:

> And my speech and my preaching was not with enticing words of man's wisdom, but in demonstration of the Spirit and of power: that your faith should not stand in the wisdom of men, but in the power of God. (1 Corinthians 2:4–5)

I have planted, Apollos watered; but God gave the increase. So then neither is he that planteth any thing, neither he that watereth; but God that giveth the increase. Now he that planteth and he that watereth are one: and every man shall receive his own reward according to his own labour. (1 Corinthians 3:6–8)

All GO! Evangelists who go out and plant the seeds of the Gospel with full dependence on the Lord's sovereign power have true joy, the assurance that God saves, and freedom.

The most blessed way in the life of a believer is to live the life of an evangelist who walks with the Holy Spirit moment by moment and sows seeds of the Gospel.

And, behold, I come quickly; and my reward is with me, to give every man according as his work shall be. (Revelation 22:12)

Chapter 8. Abundant Evangelism Opportunities

The most urgent and important reason why God urged me to write this book is that the GO! Evangelism seminars I have served during the last several years, training and challenging believers in hundreds of churches all over the United States, were not enough to train enough evangelists on time.

Now, many saints who will read this book will rise up like fire from all over the country without delay with the mission of saving souls and sow the seeds of the Gospel with joy and boldness to many lost souls around them.

The Holy Spirit will challenge all the saints who read and understand the contents of this book, and He will prepare and equip you as faithful evangelists with far more beneficial and powerful contents than the contents of the seminars of three days and two nights hosted by the churches.

The GO! Evangelism Ministry maintains an inventory over two million GO! tracts in over 50 languages, in twelve to twenty-four pages each, armed with about 1,300 words, and is fully prepared to support all GO! Evangelists immediately. Over the past few years, God has granted abundant blessings and grace to actually plant over ten million GO! tracts across the country.

Read the various evangelism cases below and pray that all of you will be raised and fully equipped as passionate GO! Evangelists.

A Golden Evangelism Opportunity Offered by Fast-Food Restaurants

I've always visited one particular fast-food restaurant in my town every Saturday morning. One morning, the restaurant is overcrowded. I park my car in the parking lot and pray to the Lord right before I get out. "Lord, whom do You want me to meet today? To what kind of souls do You want me to witness the Gospel? Lord, prepare their hearts, and save all those who will lose their chance of salvation and go to hell if they don't hear the Gospel in this restaurant today."

When I open the restaurant door and enter, I first go to the counter and say good morning to greet the staff, and I order coffee. The moment I pick up the coffee, I am now proudly a customer of this restaurant, and the employees recognize this evangelist as a customer, and they say good morning to me as well.

I go round each table and lightly greet customers as I make eye contact with them with a cheerful "Good morning." I set my coffee down on an empty table and pick up tracts. Then I go to the first table and start a conversation with a pleasant smile. "Good morning!" A young woman having breakfast with her young son welcomes this evangelist with a smile. "I have good news for you!" "Thank you!" she replies. The woman who received the tract smiles and examines the contents. "I hope to see you in heaven one day. God bless you!" "Oh, thank you! God bless you too!"

I head to the next table of the family of four who are having a meal while smiling happily and talking. "Good morning! May

I share good news with you?" Husband, wife, and two children welcome me with a smile. "May I ask you a question?" "Yes, sure!" the husband readily responds. "If you die tonight, are you going to heaven?" Since it is early in the morning, what kind of rude question is this? But the husband's reply is serious. "Well, I am not sure."

"What about you, ma'am?" I ask his wife sitting next to him. His wife also responds with a serious expression. "You know? I've never thought about it."

If God calls these unsaved couple today, they are destined for eternal destruction, but they give an answer that they are not even prepared to answer about their destiny. Two children sitting next to each other raise their hands and ask for children tracts.

The Greatest Love Story—Children's GO! Tracts

The tract for children is a GO! tract designed for a very special purpose. It is a kids' Gospel tract that contains the core of the Gospel with almost no letters and with twenty pages of colorful pictures presenting the core of the Gospel.

A tract for young children began when I read a shocking study from the Christian research organization Barna Research Report. According to the Barna Research Report, the average age of 85 percent of American Christians when they first accepted Jesus Christ as Savior and Lord was between four and fourteen years old.

This statistic is very similar to the research results of the International Bible Society, and it tells us that the heart of children is the fertile ground for the Gospel. As we get older, the heart field becomes hard and turns into a stone field, which is clearly demonstrated by the following statistics. Consider this sad reality:

- Only 10 percent of those who heard the Gospel between the ages of 15 and 30 receive Jesus Christ as their Lord and Savior.

- Only 4 percent of people over the age of 30 open their heart to the Gospel.

As I hand out the tracts *The Greatest Love Story!* to young children, I always pray: "Lord, help these little ones to meet You as they read the tract and live their lives as children of God." I say, "I want to see all of you in heaven one day." They respond, "Thank you! God bless you!" And I say, "God bless you too!"

All GO! Gospel tracts are available at the following GO! Ministry websites:

www.ChildrenTracts.com

www.GospelTracts.org

www.BibleTracts.org

Street Evangelism on the Hollywood Boulevard in Los Angeles

Two of us went out on the streets to Los Angeles Hollywood Boulevard. Among the many people we met along the way were also many tourists from European and Asian countries. We handed out many GO! tracts as we greeted them with a smile,

"Good morning! I have good news for you!" Almost everyone received the GO! tract with a smile.

We always continue evangelism while meditating on the following words from the Lord.

> And my speech and my preaching was not with enticing words of man's wisdom, but in demonstration of the Spirit and of power: that your faith should not stand in the wisdom of men, but in the power of God. (1 Corinthians 2:4–5)

> I have planted, Apollos watered; but God gave the increase. So then neither is he that planteth any thing, neither he that watereth; but God that giveth the increase. Now he that planteth and he that watereth are one: and every man shall receive his own reward according to his own labour. (1 Corinthians 3:6–8)

We do our best to plant the seeds of the Gospel in the countless people we meet whenever we do street evangelism. Because it is God who produces the fruit of the Gospel, we plant the seeds of the Gospel with joy, believing in the Lord who will bear the fruit of the Gospel abundantly.

While we were doing street evangelism on Hollywood Boulevard for three to four hours, suddenly a White man across the street waved his arm and asked us to wait for him there.

As soon as the signal changed, he just ran towards us. Overjoyed, he said he couldn't be happier when he saw the words, "Jesus' Dream Team" on our hats.

He was a pastor in the Midwest and was on vacation here in California. He was extremely happy to see us evangelizing in Hollywood, where there are many adversaries, and he was so grateful that he wanted to say hello.

Street Evangelism in Downtown Los Angeles by our GO! Ministry Team Members

Since it was a special day for street evangelism in the downtown of the city of Los Angeles, in which nearly fifty members participated, a lot of preparation was required. First, we prepare at least five thousand tracts to be planted as the seeds of the Gospel. We expect each evangelist to plant about one hundred tracts each. We also prepare hundreds of water bottles in case anyone becomes thirsty while walking on the street.

Street evangelism starts around 11 a.m. and runs for three hours until 2 p.m. Each person works with a partner to distribute tracts to everyone they meet on the pre-allocated street in downtown. When the evangelists return to the downtown park after three hours of evangelism, their happy faces are overflowing with joy and gratitude from the Lord. It is a time to sit around the lawn of the park together and share the grace we experienced while evangelizing for the past three hours. As we share the grace of God, we meditate on the excited passage in Luke 10 of Jesus' disciples returning from the field of evangelism with joy and reporting to the Lord.

Excited Evangelists Reporting to Jesus

And the seventy returned again with joy, saying, Lord, even the devils are subject unto us through thy name.

And he said unto them, I beheld Satan as lightning fall from heaven. Behold, I give unto you power to tread on serpents and scorpions, and over all the power of the enemy: and nothing shall by any means hurt you. Notwithstanding in this rejoice not, that the spirits are subject unto you; but rather rejoice, because your names are written in heaven. (Luke 10:17–20)

Delicious Hamburger Evangelism

One fast-food restaurant that I often visit during lunch time is a golden fishing ground of evangelism. Compared to other hamburger restaurants, not only does the food taste very good, but the restaurant is also cheap and clean, and the friendly service of the friendly staff who work with a sense of ownership in a restaurant always makes a splash.

This particular restaurant is an American regional chain of fast-food restaurants with locations primarily in California and the Southwest. It was founded in Baldwin Park, California. The chain has expanded outside southern California into the rest of California, as well as into Arizona, Nevada, Utah, Texas, Oregon, and Colorado, and it is planning an expansion into other states. The management philosophy of this restaurant is simple. It is about using the freshest and highest quality ingredients, always maintaining an eye-popping cleanliness, and serving guests with friendly services.

At the bottom of the drinking cup in this restaurant, you can see a Bible verse containing the essence of the Gospel.

For God so loved the world, that he gave his only begotten Son, that whosoever believeth in him should not perish, but have everlasting life. (John 3:16)

This verse proclaims a powerful message to all of us. "Right now, you are thirsty and drink the drink from this cup, but if you are saved through these words of Jesus Christ, you will drink the living water and will never thirst again." This is the crystallization of love that exquisitely contains the prayers of believers who long for all customers to become children of God.

Even at lunchtime today, I head to a fast-food restaurant near the company to preach the Gospel of the salvation of Jesus Christ, the only way of life that can forever quench the thirst for God that is deeply rooted in everyone's soul. "I have good news for you!"

I smile and walk over to the first table and start a conversation. "Good afternoon, may I share good news with you?" "Yes, of course!" Three ladies respond positively. I hand out the prepared GO! tracts, and they smile and accept the tracts and say, "Thank you!"

Businessmen Eagerly Receive GO! Tracts

At the next table, three businessmen greet me with mouths full of hamburgers and cover their mouths with their hands. "Gentlemen, could I share good news with you?" They all smile and say thank you and receive the tracts.

At the next table, four middle-aged White people stare at the evangelist warmly as they dine. "Gentlemen, could I share good news with you?" One of them jumped up from his seat with a welcome expression on his face, grabbed my hand, and said, "God bless you! We are ministers of nearby churches, but we are very grateful for courageous evangelists like you." They ask me to "keep witnessing the Gospel like this."

I head to the next table while listening to the voice of God given to our evangelists in these last days.

A Woman of God

At the next table, two middle-aged White women greet me. The woman in front says, "I am a born-again Christian. How would it be if I had the courage to evangelize like you?" Then she asked a question, "Do you know Brother Win, the evangelist in China?" She said, "You looked a lot like the Brother Win I saw in the picture." Perhaps she thinks I look similar because I am Asian. "Isn't my figure a lot better-looking?" When I joke that I know him well through the books he wrote, she asks, "Have you heard the earnest prayer requests that Brother Win offers to God these days?" When I said that I didn't know about the recent situation, the woman told me that she read an article like this a few days ago.

> Lord, do not allow the persecution against Christians in my homeland of China to disappear. In the midst of persecution and severe hardship, the Chinese church now has revival and growth with passionate love for the Lord in their hearts. Please do not stop persecution so that this image of firm faith and thorough obedience toward the Lord can continue until the day when the Lord comes.

After Brother Win escaped from China and fled to Germany, he was deeply shocked as he saw the sad reality of churches in Western countries that were collapsing. He has seen the churches in a deep spiritual sleep. So Brother Win continues to pray to the Lord like this. "Please do not stop the persecution against Christians in my homeland China. Please do not stop persecution so that they can keep their faith, which has been revitalized and grown with passionate love for the Lord in their hearts, until the day when the Lord comes."

The Chinese churches are experiencing revival and growth despite serious crises and persecution, but regrettably, they are becoming spiritually corrupt as capitalism enters at a time when they are positioned as outposts for world evangelization. I thank the Lord for giving me the opportunity to listen to the current situation of Brother Win through a White woman who confessed to being born-again Christian whom I met at a restaurant where I stopped by for evangelism today at lunchtime.

Many People Are Reading the Seeds of the Gospel

I pass all the tracts around the other dozen tables, and as I leave, I look back. When I see many people who have received the seeds of the Gospel reading the tracts, a calming feeling arises. "Lord, thank You for leading me to be used as an instrument of the Gospel today." I think to myself, "How happy our Father in heaven would be if all the members of the American church could do this easy and joyful evangelism."

As long as you believe that the Holy Spirit is the one who opens the heart of one soul and gives salvation, and you go out and deliver the GO! tract containing the core of the Gospel, then God, who is the subject of evangelism, accomplishes the work of salvation.

The words that our evangelists always memorize and meditate on are the words of 1 Corinthians 2:4: "And my speech and my preaching was not with enticing words of man's wisdom, but in demonstration of the Spirit and of power."

Evangelism that pleases the Lord is not going and persuading, but rather going and preaching what the only God, the only and almighty Sovereign of all things, has decided when He said, "I will do this." It is the responsibility of our evangelists to pick up the tract and plant the seeds of the Gospel, and here is the mission of the evangelist.

We GO! Evangelists were very brave enough to be totally ignorant.

About thirty of our GO! Evangelists gathered at the parking lot in the morning to evangelize the large shopping mall crowd in southern California. We formed a circle, held hands, prayed, and headed inside. I think we were all very brave because we were all ignorant. The shopping mall was full of people, and we started planting the seeds of the Gospel in people who were busy walking around every floor. We were evangelizing to hundreds of people for almost thirty minutes.

Two people in business shirts and ties stopped in front of me and asked questions.

"Are you the leader of this group?" When I said yes, he said, "Right now, gather all those who have come to this shopping mall with you. All your movement has been recorded in our office, and we know exactly what you guys are doing."

One of the sisters who evangelized the most passionately among us was stationed by the escalator and was passing out tracts to everyone coming down and going up, and she also gathered with us. This gentleman from the mall management was giving advice to all of us gathered in one place with a very serious expression. "Did you know that this shopping mall is private property? We cannot allow you to distribute religious material here, because this act may disturb the shoppers." His admonition was very cold and almost commanding. He continued. "If you are found here again, we will call the police."

As mentioned above, we were very brave because we were ignorant. A very interesting twist happened shortly after management left. A White middle-aged woman approached us. "First of all, I would like to thank all of you who came to evangelize. From the moment you entered this mall, I was watching you guys with concern, because I knew the management staff would soon show up. I am a retired missionary, and I have a lot of experience in this field. Hide the tracts in your pocket and dodge the security officers in the mall very stealthily. God bless you!"

Evangelism on the Busy Street of Hollywood Boulevard

The next Saturday, we evangelized on Hollywood Boulevard, which is said to be the busiest area in the city of Los Angeles. This time, around forty evangelists gathered at a fast-food restaurant to have lunch, pray together, and go out on the street. Saturday is always a busy time. Tourists from all over the world are so busy that they run into one another. We are planting the seeds of the Gospel in hundreds of people.

Suddenly, a policeman appeared in front of me. He said, "I'm warning you! You're disturbing the tourists and shop owners now, and I'll arrest you if you come back again next Saturday." It was an absurd remark, but it was probably the store owners who complained about us. But I am truly grateful that they gave us time, rather than arresting us on the spot.

Through this experience, I realized again and again that evangelism is truly a spiritual warfare. What I am really grateful for is that if our evangelists are caught doing evangelism in an underground church in China, they will be beaten and suffer all sorts of hardships and persecutions. Satan's snare is slowly coming down here in America, but the Lord makes us realize that now is the time to go out boldly and plant seeds of the Gospel to many lost souls while we still have time.

GO! Evangelists in Various Hawaiian Islands

Hawaii is brimming with tourists. Dozens of sisters living in Hawaii plant the seeds of the Gospel in hundreds of tourists every weekend. Planting seeds of the Gospel among tourists from many countries from all over the world, these sisters say that Hawaii is the golden fishery of the Gospel. Their testimonies are numerous. While meeting many tourists and planting the seeds of the Gospel, they evangelize with the regret that, in their opinion, this may be the first and last opportunity for most of these tourists to receive the Gospel.

These evangelists plant the seeds of the Gospel while always giving thanks to the Lord. "It is a testimony of how grateful and happy we are, knowing that we sow the seeds of the Gospel, water with prayer, and know that God saves those souls."

Their testimonies are the same. "We testify of the Gospel to the souls gathered from all over the world, but in the hearts of our evangelists who long for and wait for the Lord who will soon descend in the air, many lost souls are still living without hearing the Gospel." It is a sad testimony.

Beware of Your Adversaries in This Time and Here in America

The members of a church in the eastern part of the United States were challenged through an evangelism seminar, and dozens of evangelists went to nearby areas to plant the seeds of the Gospel. We were planting seeds of the Gospel while visiting a shopping center in a nearby area, and some shopkeepers came out and asked us to stop evangelizing in this area.

We were planting the seeds of the Gospel that are essential to all of them, and I could not understand why they were telling us not to do it. After an hour or two, we could clearly see the obvious reason. Suddenly, two sheriff's cars pulled up in front of us and stopped. A police officer came out of the car and gave us an absurd reason: "This is a Jewish community, so unless evangelism is stopped here immediately, I will arrest you." It was really crazy. Are they not blocking the way of salvation on their own?

Our limited time left is not enough time to care for the enemies of the Gospel like this. There are many lost souls around us who are so thirsty for the Gospel.

And he said unto them, Go ye into all the world, and preach the gospel to every creature. (Mark 16:15)

This Era of Persecution Is Slowly but Surely Coming to America as Well

In Mark 16:15, street evangelism is seen as a commandment from Jesus as a way to warn perishing souls about sins and their consequences. The recent Evangelical Leaders Survey asked U.S. evangelical leaders about their experience with persecution and their projections for the future. While only 32 percent indicated that they have been actually persecuted for their Christian faith, 76 percent expect there will be more persecutions in coming years.

Jesus warned that the world will be filled with all kinds of evil in these last days, when the Lord's Second Coming is approaching minute by minute. Jesus warned us that people would be engrossed in worldly complacency, success, and pleasure. Eventually, they would become helpless in the face of the sudden judgment, so the Lord told us to stay awake. All the saints should go out on the road without delay and sow the seeds of the Gospel in many lost souls, as we are running out of time.

Take ye heed, watch and pray: for ye know not when the time is. (Mark 13:33)

Jobber Market Attracts Thousands of Wholesale Buyers from All Over the World

On Saturday mornings, Jobber Market in downtown Los Angeles attracts thousands of people from all over the world. This also is a golden fishing ground of evangelism.

In order to sow the seeds of the Gospel to thousands of people within a few blocks in a short time, I have to move very quickly and sow the seeds of the Gospel while shouting, "Jesus loves you!" Shoppers also come to buy new things at wholesale, so they, too, are very busy and gratefully receive the seeds of the Gospel. In the first hour, the seeds of the Gospel were planted in more than five hundred people. This Jobber Market ends as fast as it gets busy. Praying that all these souls will be saved through the seeds of the Gospel and the power of the Holy Spirit, I then drive to the next area, which takes an hour by the freeway.

Numerous Elderly Seniors Having Breakfast at Fast-Food Restaurants

On the way to the next neighborhood where many shopping centers are located, I turn on the navigation of the car and input the fast-food restaurant chain with the most number of restaurants in the vicinity. I visit all six restaurants in this area.

At the first table, an elderly couple is sitting and having breakfast. "Good morning! I'd like to share good news with you." The couple receives the tracts very warmly and greets me with a comment: "Hey, you are planting the seeds of the Gospel, aren't you?"

Every time I meet such a believer, I can't tell you how grateful I am for the fullness of joy the Lord gives me. However, there are also many people who do not respond to the Gospel at all and have completely lifeless expressions. I can't tell you how sad it is to meet lost souls who have no joy or emotion. It is impossible to express how pitiful the souls are who live a dull life without hope or joy of heaven or fear of hell.

Some people raise their voices with a bored expression. "I don't care, so please pass on the tract to other people" is their sad response. I am deeply saddened to think that I will miss out on this precious opportunity to sow the seeds of the Gospel to save one soul at this precious time on this Saturday morning. It is painful to think that this opportunity may be the last chance the Lord gives this soul.

> We then, as workers together with him, beseech you also that ye receive not the grace of God in vain. (For he saith, I have heard thee in a time accepted, and in the day of salvation have I succoured thee: behold, now is the accepted time; behold, now is the day of salvation.) (2 Corinthians 6:1–2)

The Joy and Mission of Evangelism Deeply Experienced by the Senior Pastor of a Nearby Megachurch

I went out to outreach with a senior pastor who works with several dozens of associate pastors, and we experienced a truly amazing grace. The area had a lot of Latino people, and I was planting the seeds of the Gospel for a while, but the senior pastor was nowhere to be seen.

After looking for a while, I found the pastor and a Latino couple sitting together on the floor at the corner of the market parking lot, reading tracts together and planting the seeds of the Gospel. The senior pastor, who rode in my car on the way back to the church after evangelizing for more than two hours, testified of the Lord's grace he received while evangelizing to dozens of people today.

"Elder Spencer, this is the first time I have personally gone out to the road to evangelize while serving as a pastor for many years. I made a promise to the Lord today, while doing field evangelism for the first time in my pastoral life, to encourage all associate pastors and church members to teach and challenge themselves to live the life of an evangelist, realizing that evangelism, the essence of the church, is our great and urgent mission."

Since then, this church has been giving joy to the Lord for the past twenty years as a faithful church planting the seeds of the Gospel to more than 100,000 people every year.

A Young and Powerful Mexican Evangelist

In the sweltering heat of summer, our evangelists went on a mission trip to a city in southern Mexico. We arrived on Thursday and finished the evangelism seminar that challenged and trained 250 members from nearby churches for two days. On Saturday afternoon, we all went out on the street to evangelize with thousands of Spanish-language tracts. After the outreach was over, we went to a nearby hill and looked down at the city, praying for the many perishing souls in this city to repent and return to the Lord. While our evangelists were interceding, a young boy came to ask for Spanish tracts, and we gave him a few copies.

This young boy, who had been reading the tract very diligently for a long time, suddenly disappeared. I was thinking, "Oh, this boy has gone home." But when I opened my eyes while praying, I saw a truly amazing and strange event taking place. Another boy was reading a tract, sitting right next to the boy. But what was even more surprising was the fact that every time I opened my eyes while praying, the number of children was increasing to three, four, or five. What was truly amazing was the testimony of this little boy. "I was reading the first Spanish tract I received, and I thought I wanted to share this good news with my friends, so I invited my close friends nearby one by one to read it together."

Over the past twenty years, I have met many people in many regions and planted many seeds of the Gospel, but it was the first time the Lord led me to see the fruits of the Gospel so immediately.

The prayer I prayed to the Lord as I left the short-term mission field was as follows:

"Lord, grant us the blessing of saving many perishing souls in this land of Mexico as these little children grow up in faith and mature as evangelists like the apostle Paul."

I have planted, Apollos watered; but God gave the increase. So then neither is he that planteth any thing, neither he that watereth; but God that giveth the increase. Now he that planteth and he that watereth are one: and every man shall receive his own reward according to his own labour. (1 Corinthians 3:6–8)

A Couple Who Devoted a Full Year to Plant the Seeds of the Gospel

This faithful couple of the Lord, who carries souls from all over the United States, goes to each state and sows the seeds of the Gospel, determined to devote a full year to God alone. In the heart of the couple, they decided to devote themselves to the Lord with determination and mission to plant the seeds of the Gospel. They prayed and prepared an RV in order to travel to hundreds of cities to testify the Gospel to souls from the western end to the eastern end of the country and went on a missionary journey with the Lord.

They called our office every three to four weeks and shared their testimonies of God's amazing work during that time with joy and emotion, and they asked us to dispatch more needed GO! tracts in thousands at a time. The victorious missionary journey continued over several months. Through this outreach trip, the expected number of souls that God prepared to receive the seeds of the Gospel was tens of thousands of people. When I talked to them on the phone every few weeks, I felt for sure that they were continuing on a journey full of passion, gratitude, and testimonies that were not exhausting at all.

Over 1.4 Million Vietnamese Immigrants in America
Wait for the Gospel of Jesus Christ

The 1.4 million Vietnamese immigrants now in the country represent one of the largest foreign-born groups in the United States and account for about 3 percent of the overall 44.5 million U.S. immigrants. Over 40 percent of the Vietnamese immigrants reside in California, concentrated in Orange, Los Angeles, and Santa Clara counties.

Texas is home to more than 210,000 Vietnamese-Americans, and a large portion have settled in Houston and the Dallas-Fort Worth metroplex, where you'll find vibrant neighborhoods celebrating their culture. The greater Houston area is home to the second-largest Vietnamese population in the country, with approximately 143,000 people. Our ministry has already shipped Vietnamese language tracts in tens of thousands of units to all over the country.

A young Vietnamese-American pastor in Houston, Texas, has just placed five thousand GO! Vietnamese Gospel tracts in order to plant the seeds of the Gospel to Vietnamese-Americans. This young pastor is evangelizing with the determination to sow the seeds of the Gospel with the emotion and conviction of God's unstoppable love.

He clearly understood God's deep sorrow for many Vietnamese perishing souls. In the heart of this passionate young pastor lies as great a concern for unbelievers as the joy of the Gospel. He clearly realized that if there is only the joy and emotion of salvation and no sorrow for those who have not been saved, the person will never be a Christian who pleases the Lord.

The Number of Korean Churches Has Increased Significantly over the Years

The number of Korean churches in the United States has increased. In particular, the Korean immigrant community is closely associated with the church, so it is a very important indicator for understanding the overall population composition.

The Korean diaspora in the U.S. is comprised of approximately 2 million individuals who were born in South Korea or North Korea or reported Korean ancestry or race, making it the twentieth-largest diaspora group in the United States.

The eleven states with the largest estimated Korean-American populations are California (452,000, 1.2 percent); New York (141,000, 0.7 percent); New Jersey (94,000, 1.1 percent); Virginia (71,000, 0.9 percent); Texas (68,000, 0.3 percent); Washington (62,400, 0.9 percent); Illinois (61,500, 0.5 percent); Georgia (52,500, 0.5 percent); Maryland (49,000, 0.8 percent); Pennsylvania (41,000, 0.3 percent); and Colorado (31,000, 0.4 percent). Hawaii was the state with the highest concentration of Korean Americans, at 1.8 percent, or 23,200 people.

According to the research, California, which has 1,375 churches, showed the largest number of Korean churches. Comparing this number to the total Korean churches in the U.S., 30.8 percent of them are concentrated in California. New York and New Jersey followed, respectively having 461 (10.3 percent) and 263 (5.9 percent) churches. These three states make up 47 percent of the total number.

Many of these Korean-American churches are already planting the seeds of the Gospel in the many lost multiracial groups around them, and the good news is that the number of churches reaching tens of thousands of souls is increasing.

The Korean churches in Korea have sent over 22,260 missionaries to over 170 countries around the world, and 1,435 missionaries of foreign nationality were also sent. According to the recently established definition, a long-term missionary is a Korean or a Korean national who has planned to do missionary work for more than two years in another culture.

There are over one thousand Chinese churches in the United States, bringing together diasporic Chinese from diverse origins—Taiwan, Hong Kong, mainland China, and Southeast Asian countries. Our ministry published GO! Gospel tracts in two Chinese language versions: a traditional and a simplified version. The difference between traditional and simplified Chinese can cause confusion when choosing the right tract version.

The first step would be to define your target audience. Are you planting the seeds of the Gospel in those who live in mainland China, Hong Kong, Taiwan, or Singapore? If you want to target Hong Kong and Taiwan, you should distribute traditional Chinese translation. On the other hand, if mainland China and Singapore are your objective, then you should opt for the simplified Chinese translation. Our ministry has already shipped these Chinese tracts all over the world in tens of thousands of units.

Pray for Christians in Mainland China amid Intense Persecutions

Churches have been persecuted, closed, and demolished. House churches have been raided, with pastors handcuffed mid-service. Christians are arrested, interrogated, and imprisoned. Crosses are removed from church buildings. A new Chinese law has led to a widespread crackdown on Christians in provinces throughout the country. Many Christians, including the Voice of the Martyrs, is actively assisting and asking all Christians to help Chinese Christians, even amid the increasingly hostile environment in China, just as we have for the past fifty years. The greatest needs continue to be our fervent prayer to encourage our brothers and sisters being viciously persecuted, and providing Bibles for spiritual strength amid intense persecution.

GO! Evangelists in India

There are several GO! Evangelist groups actively planting seeds of the Gospel in India. The total number of seeds planted in recent years exceeds 100,000 units. The region Kerala represents the largest Christian population at 6.14 million (18.4 percent of state population); Majority in Nagaland at 87.9 percent; Mizoram at 87.2 percent; and Meghalaya at 74.6 percent. Plurality in Manipur at 41.3 percent and Arunachal Pradesh at 31 percent. Significant populations in Goa at 25.1

percent; Pondicherry at 10.8 percent; and Tamil Nadu at 6.2 percent. Pradesh at 31 percent. Significant populations in Goa at 25.1 percent; Pondicherry at 10.8 percent; and Tamil Nadu at 6.2 percent.

Most of India's population practices either Hinduism or Islam. But Christianity has nearly 32 million followers, making it the third-largest religion in the country. Given that India has well over a billion people, this amounts to only around 2 percent of the population. A current statistic will surprise you. The percentage of Christians, according to records in Telugu states including Andhra Pradesh and Telangana, is hardly 2.5 percent. But in reality, as per any statistic, it would be not less than 25 percent. Is it not astonishing? In this region, the percentage of people who go to churches and worship Jesus Christ is 25 percent. GO! Evangelism Ministry has shipped over 100,000 units of GO! tracts in Telugu language to the region, and many local Christians have planted the seeds of the Gospel.

GO! Evangelist in Australia

A GO! Evangelist who has been planting seeds of the Gospel in the Southern Central part of Australia for the last several years recently ordered over five thousand GO! tracts, including Vietnamese, Hindi, Arabic, Korean, and English rapture tracts.

The recent Australian census data showed that 44 percent of Australians classify themselves Christian. Christian majorities were found in Queensland (56.03 percent) and New South Wales (55.18 percent), while the lowest proportion of Christians were found in the Northern Territory (47.69 percent) and the Australian Capital Territory (45.38 percent).

The major denominations are as follows: Catholic, Anglican, United Church, Presbyterian, Reformed, Eastern Orthodox, Baptist, and Lutheran. The two major denominations, Anglican and Catholic, account for 36 percent of the Australian population.

GO! Evangelists in Canada

A GO! Evangelist in Canada who has been planting seeds of the Gospel very actively has ordered another twelve thousand units to be distributed. She started planting the seeds of the Gospel several years ago and consistently purchases twelve thousand units every year.

Our most recent survey in Canada found that a slim majority of Canadian adults (55 percent) say they are Christian, including 29 percent who are Catholic and 18 percent who are Protestant.

About 30 percent of Canadians say they are either atheist (8 percent), agnostic (5 percent), or "nothing in particular" (16 percent). Canadian census data indicate that the share of Canadians in this "religiously unaffiliated" category rose during the last thirty years, from 4 percent to 24 percent, although it is lowest in Quebec. In addition, a rising share of Canadians identifies with other faiths, including Islam, Hinduism, Sikhism, Judaism, and Buddhism, due in large part to immigration.

GO! Evangelists in England

We have several GO! Evangelists in England actively planting the seeds of the Gospel. The religion that the largest proportion of the populations in both England and Wales identified with was Christianity (59 percent and 58 percent, respectively). Sadly, during the last ten years, the Muslim population has increased almost ten times faster than the non-Muslim population. Islam is the fastest growing religion in the United Kingdom, and its adherents have the lowest average age out of all the major religious groups.

Wider recent research suggests that Britain is becoming more secular not because adults are losing their religion or inclination to practice but because elderly people with an attachment to the Church of England and other Christian denominations are gradually being replaced in the population by unaffiliated younger people.

Global GO! Evangelists

Every time we receive orders for GO! Gospel tracts from evangelists in the United States through our ministry website, we are very happy, but when we receive orders for tracts from many foreign countries, we are really thankful to the Lord for the privilege to serve. The languages they order are quite diverse: English, Spanish, Korean, Chinese, Hebrew, Javanese, Arabic, Bengali, Burmese, Cambodian, French, German, Haitian, Hakka, Hausa, Igbo, Indonesian, Italian, Javanese, Marathi, Pashto, Polish, Punjabi, Portuguese, Russian, Swahili, Tagalog,

Tamil, Telugu, Thai, Turkish, Ukrainian, Urdu, Vietnamese, and Yoruba, including children's tracts and others.

All of the evangelists who order directly from these various regions are evangelizing in the region where the language is spoken. Sending missionaries to these various areas requires intensive training and a huge cost. However, the native evangelists who live in this area can use the knowledge and fluent language they have accumulated during their lives to evangelize. As we think about how powerful the tools of the Holy Spirit will be, it makes us extremely happy, excited, and thankful.

The Mission of This Age Given to Our GO! Evangelists

We are now living in an era in which international migration and exchanges around the world are rapidly increasing year by year, amid a wave of globalization unprecedented in history.

God has scattered all the peoples of the world to all corners of the world, leading tens of millions of people to live the life of the diaspora. The history of the world has been changed and developed by active diasporas. Diasporas, people groups living scattered around the world, can be said to be the secret recipients of the Gospel provided and prepared by God. According to a U.N. report, about 200 million people around the world migrate every year. More than 45 million of them live here in the United States.

Muslims, Hindus, and Buddhists, known as mission populations in which the persecution against Christians is increasing and whom missionaries are reluctant to engage, have come to the United States for various reasons and live together.

Various races from all over the world are living the American Dream. The lost souls gathered from many different cultures would never have had the opportunity to have access to the Gospel if they had stayed living in their own country. Now, for us evangelists living in America, a golden opportunity to spread the Gospel to these countless perishing souls is wide open.

GO! Tracts in over 50 Languages: The Powerful Tool for Multiracial Evangelism

Of the more than 45 million immigrants living in the United States, there are over 27 million Hispanics, over 8 million Muslims, over 2 million Buddhists, and 2 million Hindus.

Most of them are concentrated in large cities, where our GO! Evangelists can easily meet and plant the seeds of the Gospel. Taking advantage of the fact that 25 percent of New Yorkers and nearly 50 percent of Los Angeles citizens speak Spanish, it is easy to reach these minorities and plant the seeds of the Gospel. In order to take advantage of this golden opportunity, the tracts that God has prepared for evangelism for multiracial groups are the GO! Evangelism tracts available at the following websites.

www.GospelTracts.org

www.BibleTracts.org

Multiracial souls who have accepted the GO! Gospel tracts continue to read with curiosity and alertness to the challenging questions that pose the problem of one's soul and existence on the cover and initial pages of the tract.

At the same time, they will come across the Gospel that offers the way to eternal life by addressing the question of death and salvation that everyone on earth fears. These questions include, "Where Will You Spend Eternity?" and "How Much Time is Left in Your Life?" The tracts also include such statements as, "You must prepare for the life after death! Time is running out fast!" "Tomorrow may be too late! The choice is yours!" "If you aren't biblically saved at this moment, you are a heartbeat away from hell!" "Eternal and unavoidable punishment in the lake of fire is waiting for you, with no hope of ever getting out!" "You must prepare for your death today! Tomorrow may be too late!"

At the conclusion, there is a prayer to receive Jesus Christ as one's Savior and Lord. There are also countless testimonies of prayers with an evangelist or alone, when the Holy Spirit, who is the Sovereign of salvation anytime and anywhere, opens a person's heart and works. In addition, GO! tracts are the pinnacle of bringing Christianity closer to atheists and people of other religions who have lived with vague curiosity about Christianity. These tracts make it possible for those who have longed for a turning point in their lives and were suffering to turn to God.

It is also important to train more missionaries and send them to the mission field. However, if you preach the Gospel through tracts to the ethnic minorities scattered here in the United States and always have opportunities to meet, it will be as effective as sending a missionary, and sometimes more effective than sending a missionary.

Additional GO! tracts are now being prepared to reach many other regions of the world that desperately need Jesus Christ.

Our GO! Evangelism Ministry continues to translate and publish tracts in many other languages listed below. Local pastors and missionaries help to translate and publish GO! tracts to reach countless perishing souls. The numbers in parentheses represent the approximate number of people worldwide who speak the language as their mother tongue.

Bhojpuri (about 33 million); Farsi (about 120 million); Gujarati (about 46 million); Kannada (about 57 million); Malayalam (about 34 million); Nepalese (about 17 million); Odiya (about 50 million); Romanian (about 29 million); Dutch (about 25 million); Sindhi (about 24 million); Sudanese Arabic (about 32 million); and more coming.

A Wealthy Woman Whom the Lord Led to Salvation

The wife of a very successful corporate president and her friends visited our house. This woman had never been to church and had never heard of the Gospel. When I prayerfully asked, "I have some really good news; would you like to hear it?" she readily agreed. I took out a GO! tract and explained it step-by-step from the beginning.

"How much time do you have left in your life? Death comes suddenly and unexpectedly! Did you know that your spirit and soul are eternal and live forever after your physical death? The Bible teaches that we consist of body, soul, and spirit. You must prepare for the life after death! Time is running out fast!"

She asked, "Is there really a life after death? Are heaven and hell real? Can I know what really happens when I die?" I invited her to slowly read what God has revealed to us:

Our creator God reveals clearly what happens when we die. As you will see, God has a plan for all who have ever lived, whether or not they knew about God during this lifetime. God who created you loves you and wants you home with Him! God gave up His Son to save you and give you the eternal life in heaven. Claim the great promise!

If you aren't certain that you are biblically saved at this moment, you are a heartbeat away from hell. Eternal and unavoidable punishment in the lake of fire is waiting for you with no hope of ever getting out! You must prepare for your death today! Tomorrow may be too late!

Hell is an everlasting burning place where there will be weeping, wailing, and gnashing of teeth, a place of regret where the smoke of those tormented goes up forever and they find no rest, day or night. You must be prepared! The Bible continuously warns us of the Day of Judgment.

The Holy God of creation hates sin, and the Day of Judgment is approaching fast. Those who live without forgiveness will have no other choice but to face the eternal damnation in the fires of hell. The choice you make now will affect your whole life and where you spend eternity.

God says, "And as it is appointed unto men once to die, but after this the judgment" (Hebrews 9:27).

Tears were welling in her eyes after reading through the entire GO! tract carefully and accurately, experiencing the entire core content of the Gospel, and she confessed that she would receive Jesus Christ as her Savior and Lord at this time and that she would be saved. Whenever I witness such a touching moment to the faithful Lord, I am grateful and give praise for saving a soul through the amazing work and power of the Holy Spirit.

The Powerful Seeds of the Gospel Change Lives!

It was a mysteriously beautiful night, full of joy and gratitude. I was on my way to my hotel after a really moving missionary meeting at which I had been all day. At a megachurch in Seoul, over three thousand missionaries from all over the world gathered in one place to hold a missionary meeting. It was after a period of traveling together with some of the evangelists doing GO! Evangelism ministry in Los Angeles, and I was attending a really meaningful missionary conference full of emotion and joy.

It was a beautiful night, with the first snow of the year coming down. The saint who drove us to the hotel was the director in charge of discipleship training at this megachurch, and he was a director of a large corporation for a living.

As an evangelist, whenever I meet such a faithful and passionate worker, I always get very curious and have a question I really want to ask: "What kind of grace did this saint receive from the Lord, that he works so passionately?" I asked the question outright. "Saint, if the Lord calls you home at this moment, are you sure 100 percent that you will go to heaven?"

The exact reason I asked this question was to hear the testimony of this saint, to be challenged, and to experience the grace of the Lord once again. But to my surprise, his answer was totally and completely unexpected. "I have been in the church for nearly thirty years so far and have done my best to take on all important ministries within the church, but I am not 100 percent sure about that question yet."

As soon as we arrived at our hotel, everyone in the party prayed with the tract in front of them, and this director began to read the contents of the seed of the Gospel. The GO! tract, the seeds of the Gospel, is the Word of God presented in about 1,300 words. As he read page by page, God's passionate impression came upon him. We all praise and testify that God has given him a precious and blessed time to testify of 100 percent assurance of salvation by praying to receive Jesus Christ as his Savior and Lord.

Another Powerful Work of God through GO! Tracts, the Seeds of the Gospel

It was an early Sunday morning. I was praying together and talking with a Sunday school director in the quiet room of the church. This church member had already completed two years of study at a nearby seminary and was just about to move up to the third year. He was a very faithful servant of the Lord who had already served for a long time as the Sunday school principal during church ministry.

Again, I really wanted to hear the story of how he met the Lord during his religious life and his testimony as a faithful servant. "If the Lord calls you right now, are you 100 percent sure that you will go to the Lord?" His answer was unexpected and surprising. He hesitated for a moment and then said, "I haven't been able to solve that problem yet." We prayed together and opened a GO! tract, presenting the seed of the Gospel again, and we began to read slowly, praying for the Lord's help. Together, we knelt on the floor of the Sunday school classroom and, with the inspiration of the Lord, this Sunday school director received the Lord as his Savior and Lord. He prayed to receive Jesus Christ as his Savior and Lord, and we both had time to experience God's abundant grace.

Personal Encounters with Many Church Members at Various Churches

During the past two decades, I have personally met many church members and asked them the same questions while leading evangelism seminars in many churches across the United States. The question I've asked was Question 1, out of five questions presented in our Evangelism Training Manual.

Question 1: If you die tonight, how certain are you that you will enjoy eternal life with God in heaven?

( ) Not quite sure ( ) 50 percent ( ) 75 percent ( ) 90 percent ( ) 100 percent

Surprisingly, more than 70 percent of the hundreds of believers who were asked this question answered 50 percent to 75 percent. Among them, some saints gave really absurd answers.

"Isn't it true that we have to die to know for sure?" Or, "Only God knows the correct answer to this question, so how can we know?"

But I discovered something really surprising. Among the hundreds of believers who were asked the same question, I found a small number of believers who confirmed 100 percent assurance of salvation every time. All of them who answered 100 percent were saints who zealously testified of the Gospel. I was able to find the answer to this wonderful reason while praying to the Lord. The secret was evangelism to save lost souls that the Lord was most pleased with!

These few evangelists were well aware that prayer, the Word, and evangelism were very important in their personal spiritual life. If prayer is the breath of the spirit, the Word is the nourishment of the spirit, and evangelism to save the soul is the movement of the spirit. The reason that the spirit was able to grow up strong and healthy was because they were witnessing the Gospel to the many perishing souls around them.

This is because they knew and were already receiving the infinite blessings given to evangelists. The infinite and abundant blessings they've been receiving were as follows:

1. They were believers who received truly divine food that the world could not imagine.

> Jesus saith unto them, My meat is to do the will of him
> that sent me, and to finish his work. (John 4:34)

What is the Father's will and the Father's work, according to the Lord? That is what it means to save countless perishing souls—that is, evangelism.

2. Second, evangelistic believers can always maintain the fullness of the Holy Spirit.

> And be not drunk with wine, wherein is excess; but be filled with the Spirit; speaking to yourselves in psalms and hymns and spiritual songs, singing and making melody in your heart to the Lord; giving thanks always for all things unto God and the Father in the name of our Lord Jesus Christ. (Ephesians 5:18–20)

3. God answers our prayers.

> If ye abide in me, and my words abide in you, ye shall ask what ye will, and it shall be done unto you. (John 15:7)

Therefore, evangelism is a necessary condition for God to answer prayers.

4. We receive the abundant blessings prepared for our evangelists.

> But seek ye first the kingdom of God, and his righteousness; and all these things shall be added unto you. (Matthew 6:33)

Dear brothers and sisters, we must evangelize and witness to the Gospel because it is the earnest heart of our beloved God.

GO! Evangelists in Northern California

The director in charge of evangelism in this church always orders five thousand GO! tracts at a time. On Saturday afternoon, the entire evangelism team gathered at the elevated bleachers of the park in downtown, chanting passionately, praying to the Lord for the salvation of the perishing souls of the city, and continuing to sing until many people gathered.

After a large number of people gathered, and the pastor testified briefly of the Gospel, it was time to plant the seeds of the Gospel in all the gathered people. Then it was time for all the evangelists to go around downtown in pairs to plant the seeds of the Gospel in all the passersby. Even today, all the evangelists who planted the seeds of the Gospel that afternoon in thousands of souls are overflowing with thanks and praise because they have the assurance that many of them will be saved by the power of God. The evangelists planted the seeds of the Gospel and watered them in prayer, but only God gave them the belief that they will grow, so they decide to continue planting the seeds of the Gospel until the day the Lord comes.

> I have planted, Apollos watered; but God gave the increase. So then neither is he that planteth any thing, neither he that watereth; but God that giveth the increase. Now he that planteth and he that watereth are one: and every man shall receive his own reward according to his own labour. (1 Corinthians 3:6–8)

Do You Have a Clear Goal in Your Life as a Faithful Christian?

To every believer living in America, the Lord asks the following questions: "What is the purpose of your life in this age?" The reason why John the Baptist was a great prophet is that he went out into the wilderness to become "the voice of one crying in the wilderness" (Matthew 3:3), wearing camel's fur, wearing a leather belt around his waist, eating locusts and sagebrush, proclaiming the truth of the kingdom, and living a sacrificial life.

Saints all over the United States should clearly understand the special and specific calling and mission of God who has planted us and made us live in this age. By taking advantage of the opportunities for devotion prepared by the Lord, we have a prophetic mission like John the Baptist and become God's spokesperson to be greatly used in the work of saving many perishing lost souls. Since the United States is a multiethnic country in which diverse races from all over the world live together in a community with the characteristics of each region's culture, it is a land of great opportunity to meet various races and to testify of the Gospel to them.

In God's great providence, our saints were sent to save the many poor souls in America who are on the path of profound spiritual corruption and destruction in these last days.

In this spiritually stagnant United States, we should all aware of the heart of our heavenly Father, who wants us to be used in the work of the Holy Spirit to cause a great spiritual awakening and save countless souls. We all have to change and mature.

> Before I formed thee in the belly I knew thee; and before thou camest forth out of the womb I sanctified thee, and I ordained thee a prophet unto the nations. (Jeremiah 1:5)

"I Ordained Thee a Prophet unto the Nations"

All of us living as believers here in the United States are absolutely chosen and called in God's absolute sovereignty and providence. What does it mean to be a prophet of the nations? It means to be an advocate of God, one who preaches and proclaims the Word of God to all nations and to souls of all races. The prophets of the nations who have been called in this way are God's prophets who have the task of rebuking all souls of the world for their sins, proclaiming God's imminent judgment, and delivering the message of awakening.

What was Jeremiah's response to God's call?

Then said I, Ah, Lord God! behold, I cannot speak: for I am a child. (Jeremiah 1:6)

When Jeremiah heard God's shocking words, "I ordained thee a prophet unto the nations," his heart fell, and he looked at himself. In that moment, instead of gratitude, joy, and emotion, he was gripped with sadness, anxiety, fear, and burden. The twenty-year-old young man who knew himself very well, who was very weak and immature, looked at himself and sighed.

When all of us believers examine ourselves objectively, the same lament is bound to come out. It is a difficult reality to make a living here in the United States, and we know too well that it would be impossible to testify the Gospel to the countless lost souls around us.

But God is speaking to us the same words in verse 7 that He said to Jeremiah.

But the Lord said unto me, Say not, I am a child: for thou shalt go to all that I shall send thee, and whatsoever I command thee thou shalt speak. (Jeremiah 1:7)

God says, "Don't call yourself incompetent."

Although we live an extremely busy and tiring life with no spare time in our lives, God, who insists on life and death, has appointed us as prophets of the nations. Therefore, we ourselves should be recognized as a prophet of the nations of the world.

A prophet established by God is not a person who speaks with his own wisdom but is an instrument of the Gospel who receives the Word of God and preaches it as it is.

And my speech and my preaching was not with enticing words of man's wisdom, but in demonstration of the Spirit and of power: that your faith should not stand in the wisdom of men, but in the power of God. (1 Corinthians 2:4–5)

God sends us to the countless lost souls; He prepares us and tells us exactly what to say. Now, more and more evangelists are boldly witnessing the Gospel to countless souls, including White people, Black people, Latino people, and all other ethnic groups who have gathered from all over the world on the street, the field of the Gospel, across the United States.

These evangelists are living with the prophetic mission that God has established in this age, and they, too, had fear and discomfort at first when they testified of the Gospel to a multiracial group. The Lord, well aware of the fear and burden of an evangelist who proclaims the Word of God to unbelievers, speaks to the evangelist even at this time.

Be not afraid of their faces: for I am with thee to deliver thee, saith the Lord. (Jeremiah 1:8)

Although Jeremiah made a decision to obey God's mission, of course, fear remained in his heart. "As my Father hath sent me, even so send I you" (John 20:21). The Lord, who sent the saints into the world, knew well the fear of the evangelists, so He promised, "I will always be with you until the end of the world." How did God help Jeremiah, who said he called himself a child? And now, how does He help us when we are hesitant and afraid to go to the field of the Gospel? God reached out and touched Jeremiah's mouth and sanctified his mouth.

Then the LORD put forth his hand, and touched my mouth. And the LORD said unto me, Behold, I have put my words in thy mouth. See, I have this day set thee over the nations and over the kingdoms, to root out, and to pull down, and to destroy, and to throw down, to build, and to plant. (Jeremiah 1:9–10)

God reached out and touched Jeremiah's mouth and sanctified his mouth. God keeps saying, "Look!" God Himself knows how precious and blessed is his mission as an advocate of God's Word, so He does not hide His excitement and expresses it as it is.

God Never Gives Up

God is looking for a servant of the Lord who prays with faith in God's work in order to execute the work that He planned and provided while turning the wheel of human history.

The saints who testify of the Gospel are those who have a prophetic mission in the world. A prophet is one who first sees and knows the wonderful works of God through God's revelations and visions, and he is a witness to the countless souls around him.

No matter what pain and difficulty God plans and executes, there must be a servant of the Lord who agrees and prays, "Yes, God! That is just and ought to be done. Do Your will!" If there is no such servant of prayer and faith that God is looking for on this earth, God does not work in heaven. A good example of this is the Book of Jonah. The Book of Jonah is a record of the repentance and revival of the city of Nineveh, located in modern-day northern Iraq.

God Never Gives Up on What He Has Planned

God planned the repentance and revival of the people of a pagan nation. And the first thing He did was to find a servant of the Lord to be used as an instrument for their salvation. This can be seen in Jonah 1.

> Now the word of the Lord came unto Jonah the son of Amittai, saying, Arise, go to Nineveh, that great city, and cry against it; for their wickedness is come up before me. (Jonah 1:1-2)

God has now decided to deal with the poor people who have only God's judgment remaining. The level of danger that the evil of the rebellious people of Nineveh has already reached the heavens, and God tells Jonah to participate in His mission.

But there is a very serious problem here. Jonah refuses to be used as an instrument of the Gospel in God's plan, and he runs away. God never gives up on what He has planned. As Jonah chapters 1–2 testifies, God finds the servant of the Lord who has fled, and He puts him in the furnace of unimaginable suffering until he realizes God's plan and participates in joy. He treats him tenaciously until he realizes himself, repents with tears, and returns. The Book of Psalms contains the confession of doing what God asks, who knows us better than ourselves and knows the blessed path we must take:

> Whither shall I go from thy spirit? or whither shall I flee from thy presence? If I ascend up into heaven, thou art there: if I make my bed in hell, behold, thou art there. If I take the wings of the morning, and dwell in the uttermost parts of the sea; even there shall thy hand lead me, and thy right hand shall hold me. (Psalm 139:7–10)

The God of love puts Jonah into the belly of a big fish, a furnace of suffering, and trains him harshly for three days and three nights.

> The waters compassed me about, even to the soul: the depth closed me round about, the weeds were wrapped about my head. (Jonah 2:5)

Jonah cries out to the Lord because of his severe suffering.

> Call unto me, and I will answer thee, and shew thee great and mighty things, which thou knowest not. (Jeremiah 33:3)

At the crossroads of life and death a large fish swallowed water and was submerged to the depths. When it exhaled, it took a short breath, and went in and out of the water for three days and three nights. Then Jonah cried out with a prayer of repentance. God desperately needed the Lord's servant to be used as an instrument in the work God had planned, even through the furnace of refinement.

Do you really know God's deep sorrow for the lost souls?

Among the multitude of people in Nineveh, where judgment was imminent, who would know God and pray to God? And who would pray for the people of an enemy country even if they are Jews who know God? I ask you the same question.

Who will have a heart to pray for this American land, where judgment is imminent?

At that time, the only person God expected was Jonah. Are you the only person God is expecting in your town?

God absolutely needs people who agree with God's plan to pray and go out to testify of the Gospel. When Jonah returned from a prayer of repentance, Nineveh's repentance and revival could be seen in an instant. Miracles on this earth can happen so easily and quickly when God moves our hearts to receive the faith, obedience, and prayer with joy, through the saints who pray and say amen to God's plan.

You are the evangelist of the prophetic mission established by God.

Today, we are living in a special and urgent time. The number of unreached people groups around the world is now shrinking, and it is a very urgent time when the Lord's Great Commission is nearing fulfillment.

> And this gospel of the kingdom shall be preached in all the world for a witness unto all nations; and then shall the end come. (Matthew 24:14)

Dear saints! Now is the time to really wake up and pray even while sleeping.

As I personally planted the seeds of the Gospel through GO! tracts for more than fifty thousand multiracial souls over the past few years, I feel extreme regret and despair. I have been to many areas in the United States, which is a Christian country, but it is almost impossible to meet an evangelist.

I shout the name of Jesus Christ out loud all afternoon on the street, the field of the Gospel, and I walk for hours and miles to spread the love of Jesus Christ to everyone I meet, but it is really difficult to find an evangelist who bears witness to the Gospel. There are countless souls who cannot but perish forever because of us. Have you ever wondered how heartbroken the Lord will be if you continue to lead an irresponsible life without concern for the souls around you entrusted to you?

As I went out on the street every week and witnessed the Gospel to hundreds of souls, I made a decision as I experienced the wonderful grace that God prepared, the tears of my heavenly

Father, and the joy of the Father toward this evangelist. Until now, all missions have been entrusted to the missionaries at the forefront of the mission field, and most of the church members are participating in the mission with prayers and materials as missionaries from the rear. So now, I am writing this book with the determination to awaken, train, challenge, build up, and send all the saints behind the missionary mission as evangelists.

From Complete Despair and Abandonment of Life to Complete New Hope and Joy

The youth GO! Evangelists of the nearby church were dedicated to planting the seeds of the Gospel in everyone they met at the nearby shopping center parking lot for about two hours before the service every Sunday morning. On that Sunday morning, this sister was a little disappointed because many people she met were negative about receiving the seeds of the Gospel, but the only way for all these people to be saved was through the Gospel of Jesus Christ, so she prayed and continued to plant the seeds of the Gospel.

At that time, a White middle-aged man in the distance was fixing his car tire under the shade of a tree. She approached him and said, "Good morning! I'd like to share good news with you!" But he did not react at all, nor did he look at her. This sister was a little disappointed and began to walk to leave the place, but suddenly this gentleman responded with a loud voice. "Did you say good news? Please continue!"

This evangelist sister began to read the GO! tract from the cover. "Are you saved? Where will you spend eternity?

How much time is left in your life? Death comes suddenly and unexpectedly. You must be prepared for the life after. Time is running out fast! If you aren't biblically saved at this moment, you are a heartbeat away from hell. You must prepare for your death today! Tomorrow may be too late!"

While she was reading the tract, the gentleman was listening very carefully to everything. Suddenly, tears welled up in his eyes and he began to sob. "Sister, I want to have a conversation with you about who I am and what I am doing here." And he couldn't hold back the tears that were flowing.

He was a member of the church in Florida, serving the church diligently with his beloved wife and children. As the business he had built over several decades went bankrupt, he became so frustrated that his life as a believer was insignificant, and he made an extreme choice. He irresponsibly dispersed his family to his relatives' houses, and he foolishly decided to commit suicide. He drove across the American continent to southern California.

On the freeway, the tire of the car he was driving suddenly exploded, and he rushed out to the exit. While he was changing his tire at the parking lot here at the shopping center, this sister who came to him began preaching the Gospel to him. While she was reading the Gospel, he kept hearing the Lord's earnest voice, "Come back."

He then made a firm decision. He decided to go back and gather all his family members and live as the believer that the Lord wants. As soon as he heard the voice of the Lord, he decided to go back. After giving thanks to this sister evangelist and turning the car back to Florida, this sister went to the church with flowing tears of gratitude for the Lord.

When the sister arrived at the church, the worship service had already begun, and all the members of the church were singing the hymn, "I will go this way until the Lord comes again." Unstoppable tears continued to flow from the sister's eyes.

The pastor, who found that the sister evangelist couldn't contain her tears while singing the hymn, approached her and asked, "What happened today?" She said, "The Lord used me as an instrument of the Gospel." The pastor asked her to testify in front of the congregation, and she testified of the miraculous work of God that happened in the field of evangelism that morning. It was a precious time to share the moving grace of God.

Now Is the Time for the Powerful New Paradigm of Evangelism

I have come to the conclusion that missions and evangelism to save souls that God has entrusted to us are impossible using the same paradigm of evangelism as before. In the meantime, many peoples and souls have been saved through dedicated missionaries.

These methods must continue until the day the Lord comes. However, there are too many perishing souls around us who cannot be saved by this approach alone. If so many born-again believers here in America plant the seeds of the Gospel in at least ten lost souls every week, how precious will they be to God in this age? Are you worried about what kind of fruit the Gospel seeds you plant will bear? You plant the seeds of the Gospel, but who said that you make them grow and bear the fruit of the Gospel? Only God promises to make it grow.

When we truly believe in the power of God and plant the seeds of the Gospel, many lost souls we could not have imagined will come back to the Lord. In heaven, there will be resounding shouts of joy among the angels.

> I have planted, Apollos watered; but God gave the increase. So then neither is he that planteth any thing, neither he that watereth; but God that giveth the increase. Now he that planteth and he that watereth are one: and every man shall receive his own reward according to his own labour. (1 Corinthians 3:6–8)

Now is the time to pray for mercy from our heavenly Father for the salvation of so many lost and perishing souls around us, to open the heavens wide, and to bring repentance and revival to this very land and city in which we all breathe.

The obedient and going Jonahs of God must arise. If you do not rise up with the Gospel, there may be no way for the millions of souls who encounter you to be saved forever. If God has entrusted the salvation of those souls to you alone, you should kneel and pray for the salvation of those souls today and listen to and obey God's voice, as He says, "Go and proclaim."

In the meantime, our churches have been praying and supporting missionaries, but they have neglected the pioneer work for the nearby cities that God has entrusted to us. If all the members of the church in which we serve now, as prophets in this area, pray for the many lost souls around us, obey God's

Word and plan, and plant the seeds of the Gospel in all the perishing souls we meet with GO tracts, the gates of heaven will open, and the work of repentance and revival will come to this land and our surrounding cities.

> And he said unto them, Go ye into all the world, and preach the gospel to every creature. (Mark 16:15)

> I charge thee therefore before God, and the Lord Jesus Christ, who shall judge the quick and the dead at his appearing and his kingdom; preach the word; be instant in season, out of season; reprove, rebuke, exhort with all longsuffering and doctrine. (2 Timothy 4:1–2)

All the saints of America, "Let's go! Let's proclaim, and let's win perishing souls!"

Many churches in the U.S. are now actively planting the powerful seeds of the Gospel.

Many churches in southern California have been planting the seeds of the Gospel very actively to several thousands of people, every month. As our GO! Evangelism Gospel tract has the power to save many lives, they hand out GO! tracts, the seeds of eternal life in many different languages, with a sincere and pleasant smile and say, "Hi, I would like to share good news with you," or simply, "Hi, I have good news for you." If they ask, "What is it about?" they tell them the truth: "It is a Gospel tract. It will show you how to get to heaven."

These churches order directly from our GO! Evangelism Ministry websites:

www.GospelTracts.org

www.BibleTracts.org

The churches in Orange County of California specialize in visiting the Westminster area, and many individuals from all over the country specialize in planting seeds of the Gospel in Vietnamese communities throughout the nation.

Do not delay! Go now and plant the powerful seeds of the Gospel!

Jeremiah, who was very weak and full of fear, was chosen and commissioned to prophesy the Word of God, and at the same time he received the word that was to be preached in his mouth. The Lord, who chose to use GO! Evangelists, also gave us GO! Evangelism tracts, armed with the core of the Gospel. Now, no matter what anyone says, we are the evangelists of the nations. What is the mission God has given us?

Our mission is the same as that given to Jeremiah and Jonah:

First, pluck, destroy, and knock down; then build and plant. Thousands of multiracial people who have gathered here in the United States from all over the world are spiritually ignorant, not humble before God, and extremely proud. They rely more on material things than God, boasting and pursuing only the illusions that the world sees. They fall into materialism and hedonism and do not seek God.

Just as Jeremiah warned of God's judgment on the nations stained with rebellious sins, we GO! Evangelists must also warn of the imminent judgment of God and urge each soul we meet to return to God. The next mission given to us is to build and plant. It is the Word of God that we must build and plant. The most serious problem in this new generation is that they are indifferent to God's Word.

> Behold, the days come, saith the Lord GOD, that I will send a famine in the land, not a famine of bread, nor a thirst for water, but of hearing the words of the LORD: And they shall wander from sea to sea, and from the north even to the east, they shall run to and fro to seek the word of the LORD, and shall not find it. (Amos 8:11–12)

The prophet Amos continued to disobey God without seeking God. However, he clearly pointed out that it will be too late for him to return to God's Word to escape His judgment.

It is said that a famine of the Word will come when the work of the Holy Spirit is extinguished and all hopes are cut off because the sinner who has left God has neglected the Word of God, rejected the voice of the Holy Spirit, and lived in denial.

The Famine of the Word Coming in These Last Days

The famine of the Word that comes in this last age, when the Gospel is more prevalent than any other age, is not due to the absence of the Bible. It is a famine that comes because people love the world and enjoy the pleasures of sin, because their spirits are blind and their hearts are closed. Because they love sin and the pleasures of the world, they are no longer interested in God's Word of truth.

The fact that there are hardly any evangelists on the streets of southern California who receive the mission of prophets and testify of the Gospel on the streets is another big factor causing the Gospel to not be witnessed. We simply cannot change the world today with weak and helpless church members who have lost the proclamation of the cross to the world.

We, the GO! Evangelists, received the mission of building and planting the Word of God in the thirsty and perishing souls. We GO! Evangelists must plant the seeds of the Gospel by always praying, whether in time or not, to all the souls we meet in the field of life, with the GO! tract. We must plant the seeds of the Gospel of salvation to poor souls who are facing the eternal judgment of God, because there is no one who preaches the Gospel.

Let's Share the Gospel with Unreached Immigrant Groups in the U.S.

Currently, there are about two hundred unreached immigrant groups in the United States to whom the Gospel has never been preached. In this sad reality, God will be very pleased if we more actively do missionary work for immigrants in the United States and carry out missionary work even to the souls of their home country through immigrant groups who have come in contact with the Gospel.

Now is the time for believers across the United States to actively sow the seeds of the Gospel in the multiracial souls who live and breathe in the same city as us. The GO! Evangelism Gospel tracts not only make it possible for all saints to evangelize with joy, but they also reaffirmed their dignity as ambassadors of the kingdom of heaven and their identity as a secret weapon of the Gospel.

The evangelization rates of the regions with the lowest evangelization rates in the world, in which currently it is almost impossible for missionaries to work, are as follows: Afghanistan (0.02 percent); Yemen (0.05 percent); Somalia (0.05 percent); Morocco (0.1 percent); Mauritania (0.16 percent); Tunisia (0.22 percent); Algeria (0.29 percent); Iran (0.33 percent); and Niger (0.4 percent). The work of the Holy Spirit is possible because the seeds of the Gospel can be planted in immigrants living in the United States.

> How then shall they call on him in whom they have not believed? and how shall they believe in him of whom they have not heard? and how shall they hear without a preacher? and how shall they preach, except they be sent? as it is written, How beautiful are the feet of them that preach the gospel of peace, and bring glad tidings of good things! (Romans 10:14–15)

How can so many lost souls hear the Gospel of salvation without an evangelist of the Gospel? For the rebellious people of Nineveh to repent, believe the Gospel, and receive salvation, they needed the evangelism of the prophet Jonah, who was called by God. Lost souls in so many places have no other way of being saved without your obedience and devotion. The Lord is waiting for you to obey and go and plant the seeds of the Gospel even at this time.

"Arise, go to Nineveh, that great city, and shout against it!"

"Arise, go, and plant the seeds of the Gospel to the many lost souls of the city in which you now live!"

Praying a Vow to God and Evangelizing At Least Ten Souls

A GO! Evangelist made a vow to the Lord that he would evangelize to more than ten people each and every day. After working hard all day for a living, it was already 11 p.m. when he got home. However, because of his promise to evangelize to more than ten people a day, he went back to a nearby market with GO! tracts in the middle of the night to evangelize to more than ten people he met at the door, and then he returned home. His testimony is that the Lord has given him an unbearable joy and a fullness of gratitude. By the time he came home, it was way past midnight, but he did not feel tired at all; rather, full of joy, he went to bed praying that the Lord would send more perishing souls tomorrow.

Even If We Meet the Adversary of the Gospel Witness

At the first table in the next restaurant I visited, a white-haired elderly man was sitting and reading a book while eating. My first impression was that he looked like a professor at a nearby university. As I headed towards the table he was sitting at, I could feel the old man's expression suddenly hardening. I approached the table and said hello.

"Good afternoon! May I—" Before I could even finish my greeting, suddenly the old man cried out with a stern look, his eyes rolling with a very annoyed look on his face.

"You are not supposed to solicit with religious materials in here. Get out! You're handing out tracts in a public place like this, are you crazy right now? Stop it now and get out!"

In my heart, whenever I encounter such adversaries, I have the heart God the Father gave to this evangelist. Feeling full of pity for him, I urgently prayed to the Lord. "Lord, please have pity that this moment will not be the last chance for this old man to hear the Gospel."

My immediate reaction to this old man is to look into his eyes and say, "Are you sure?" Because I feel very sorry for him to think that this opportunity that the Lord is giving him now may be his last chance to be saved.

According to the words of 2 Corinthians, the fact that I am standing here now is the grace of God and his golden opportunity to be saved. How many times will he regret missing today's precious last chance of salvation while burning and suffering in hell?

We then, as workers together with him, beseech you also that ye receive not the grace of God in vain. (For he saith, I have heard thee in a time accepted, and in the day of salvation have I succoured thee: behold, now is the accepted time; behold, now is the day of salvation.) (2 Corinthians 6:1–2)

Occasionally, whenever I encounter these adversaries, I gain new courage and strength by meditating on the following words.

Blessed are ye, when men shall revile you, and persecute you, and shall say all manner of evil against you falsely, for my sake. Rejoice, and be exceeding glad: for great is your reward in heaven: for so persecuted they the prophets which were before you. (Matthew 5:11–12)

Blessed are ye, when men shall hate you, and when they shall separate you from their company, and shall reproach you, and cast out your name as evil, for the Son of man's sake. Rejoice ye in that day, and leap for joy: for, behold, your reward is great in heaven: for in the like manner did their fathers unto the prophets (Luke 6:22–23)

On the day of Pentecost, when the Holy Spirit came and many wonders and signs appeared because of the apostles, the high priest and the individual factions of the priests were filled with envy. They arrested the apostles and put them in prison, and they strictly forbid them to teach or preach in the name of Jesus. The amazing reaction of the apostles after they were severely scourged and set free can be seen in Acts chapter 5.

And to him they agreed: and when they had called the apostles, and beaten them, they commanded that they should not speak in the name of Jesus, and let them go. And they departed from the presence of the council, rejoicing that they were counted worthy to suffer shame for his name. And daily in the temple, and in every house, they ceased not to teach and preach Jesus Christ. (Acts 5:40–42)

The saints who have experienced persecution while evangelizing know the thrill and joy that the Lord has recognized them as faithful servants who are insulted for the sake of the name of Christ. We GO! Evangelists always praise the Lord who has given us this glory and privilege. We pray for all the saints of this age to become mature believers who enjoy the joy and glory of being tested in the field as servants of the Lord and recognized by the Lord.

The Lord Showing the Actual Fruits of the Gospel

It was a day not long after one of our staff delivered the GO! tract, a powerful tool of the Gospel, to the countless people he met on the road. A young man approached him and said, "I received grace while reading and meditating on the tract I received from you several days ago. At the end of the tract, I meditated on the suggested prayer to accept Jesus Christ as my Savior and Lord. I want to accept Jesus Christ as my Savior and Lord at this time; can you help me?"

Emotions that cannot be expressed in words came flooding in, leading to a prayer for him, "I pray in Jesus' name," and when he opened his eyes, there was another young man standing right behind the young man and waiting. The evangelist was surprised and curious, so he asked, "What can I do for you?" The young man's answer shocked the evangelist. "I want to do the same thing he just did." This evangelist led two young men to accept Jesus Christ on the busy street in downtown, and his heart overflowed with gratitude and praise.

Sharing Gospel Message with a Latino Family

A GO! Evangelist who regularly visits downtown parks with dozens of GO! tracts every Saturday went out to evangelize even though he had no Spanish language skills other than "burrito" and "taco." Under the shade of a tree in the park, a Latino family of five, who seemed to have just immigrated, were sitting around.

This evangelist approached them, greeted them with a broad smile, and sat down next to them. After giving out Spanish tracts to all of his family, this evangelist began to read from the cover page by page in broken Spanish, stuttering like a kindergartener reading for the first time. At that moment, the father of the family, who was listening to the poor Spanish reading and stuttering, said he would read it. He read the tract with fluent Spanish pronunciation. This evangelist was praying earnestly for God to have compassion on this family and for the family to be saved while the father of the family was reading the tract. The mom and three children listened intently while the dad read the tract in fluent Spanish.

He kept on reading about the love of God, about sin and death, about the eternal punishment of hell, and the fact that Jesus Christ died on the cross and rose again to atone for our sins, in which we are bound to perish forever, and that only the Lord can save us.

It was the only way to be saved. But when the father read John 3:16, tears began to well up in the mother's eyes. The children, who had been watching their mother for a long time, looked at their father's face with a surprised expression as he was reading the tract, and he was also reading the last page with tears in his eyes. After the dad finished reading the tract, the children looked at the dad and mom, who were wiping away tears, and they also burst into tears. This evangelist invited them, "Will you receive the Lord?" All of the family members responded that they would, and tears welled up in the eyes of this evangelist who led the reception prayer.

Now is the accepted time; behold, now is the day of salvation. (2 Corinthians 6:2)

The Power of the Gospel to Deliver a Man from Despair

Another GO! Evangelist leaves home early on Sunday morning and stops on the way to church. She stops to testify of the Gospel by stopping at a shopping center located near the church and giving out GO! tracts to everyone she meets for an hour.

Even that morning, she handed out the tracts to many people, but she was getting rejected from time to time by several people, and she was walking to the place where she parked her car in a bit of disappointment. She saw a man squatting down in front of an old car and changing a flat tire. That morning many people had refused to receive tracts, so she didn't feel very well, but thinking that the Lord might have sent her here for that one soul, she approached him and said, "Good morning, I have good news for you!" He raised his head, looked up at the evangelist, and said, "You said good news? Please continue reading while I replace this flat tire." The evangelist began to read the GO! tract.

"Where will you spend eternity? Are you saved? How much time do you have left in your life? You must prepare for the life after death! You must prepare for your death today! Tomorrow may be too late! Time is running out fast. God, who created you, loves you and wants you home with Him!"

That was the moment. A middle-aged white man, crouching in front of a tire, listening to the Gospel, suddenly started sobbed and said, "You are an angel sent to me by God," explaining why he was sitting here at this hour.

He was a believer who attended and served the church diligently. However, when the business he was running went bankrupt, the family broke up, and he fell into disappointment, and he decided to cross this nation one last time and leave this world. However, while he was driving on the freeway, the front tire suddenly punctured, so he rushed out of the next exit and entered a shopping center that caught his eye, and he was changing the tires when the evangelist found him.

He had already heard the voice of the Lord saying, "Turn back!" while this evangelist was reading the good news. The middle-aged man thanked this evangelist with tears, and he said, "Thank you so much!" over and over again, promising that he would go back across the continent to find the family he had abandoned and restore the family to serve the Lord.

When this evangelist arrived at the church, the service had already begun and the entire congregation was singing a song, and the title of the song was, "I will walk this way until the Lord comes again." Tears of emotion and gratitude flowed endlessly from the eyes of this evangelist who sang this praise together with the church.

Good News Proclaimed in Mexico

This is the unforgettable testimony of the evangelists who went on a short-term mission to a city in southern Mexico. Short-term missionaries serve in various ministries, including GO! Evangelism seminars, for local church workers, and they mobilize all-out street evangelism into the city streets.

We planted the powerful seeds of the Gospel in almost ten thousand people with the GO! Evangelism Spanish tracts we prepared, together with dozens of ministers who completed the GO! Evangelism seminar. At the place where we hold Sunday worship with the members of the local church, a sister read aloud the GO! tract and suddenly wept and was blessed to participate in the amazing work of salvation to receive Jesus Christ as her Savior and Lord.

It has been four months since we returned from a short-term mission to southern Mexico. We have received a surprising news from the church we served. The news was that the church with 600 attendees had soared to 1,200 members in just a few months. The testimonies of the new members of the church were, "I was touched by God while reading and meditating on the GO! Gospel tract I received on the street last summer, and I came to the church while realizing the need for a life of faith."

Our faithful God urged us to plant the seeds of the Gospel, watered them with our prayers, and made them bear the fruit of the Gospel with the power of God.

He made the Gospel seeds that we faithfully sow to return with abundant fruit, and He even promised that each of us would be rewarded according to our faithful work.

I have planted, Apollos watered; but God gave the increase. So then neither is he that planteth any thing, neither he that watereth; but God that giveth the increase. Now he that planteth and he that watereth are one: and every man shall receive his own reward according to his own labour. (1 Corinthians 3:6–8)

Testimony of a Sister Engaged in Street Evangelism for the First Time in Her Life

A middle-aged sister, who was passionately engaged in street evangelism, couldn't contain her emotions and ran to testify. "I have been serving as an official in the church for many years, and I have done my best, but this is the first time that I have witnessed the Gospel like this in the street."

The sister sat in a park chair with a woman and her daughter who had been out shopping and read the GO! tract from the beginning. Suddenly, tears welled up in the mother's eyes, and she was determined to accept Jesus Christ as her Savior and Lord. The evangelist said that she had prayed for their reception; she said, "God has used me as an instrument of the Gospel," and tears welled up.

Even more wonderful is that her daughter, who was listening to the Gospel with her mother, also shed tears and accepted the Lord with her mother. It was the moment when I heard the cheers of the heavenly angels looking at this moving moment of blessing.

Likewise, I say unto you, there is joy in the presence
of the angels of God over one sinner that repenteth.
(Luke 15:10)

Have you ever thought about the salvation of countless perishing souls walking by your side as you walk down the street?

Pastor Billy Graham was once asked this question: "When
did you experience the biggest spiritual crisis in your life?"
Pastor Billy Graham answered, "I have been evangelizing and
preaching the Word to people and tribes all over the world. But
I just ignored the people I always met in the markets and streets
of the same city closest to me. When I found myself passing by
the countless people without any interest, I thought it was my
biggest spiritual crisis."

Even at this hour, our heavenly Father asks this question
of the saints: "Do you have this tormented heart and love of
Mine for the lost souls around you?" Do you have any interest
and love for the lost souls you encounter every day around you?
Because in the area where you live, there is no one other than
you to plant the GO! tract containing the core of the Gospel and
to deliver the love of God.

If you can plant the seeds of the Gospel in a thousand
perishing souls throughout your life, God acknowledges that
even if you do not go to seminary and do pastoral work, and if
you cannot dedicate yourself as a missionary to the indigenous
peoples of South America and Africa, nevertheless He will

recognize your life as a good and faithful missionary whom He is pleased with.

> And they that be wise shall shine as the brightness of the firmament; and they that turn many to righteousness as the stars for ever and ever. (Daniel 12:3)

Blessings for Those Who Boldly Preach Jesus Christ

Passionately witnessing the Gospel of salvation is a shortcut to directly experiencing the power of the Holy Spirit working for the salvation of souls and equipping yourself spiritually. Evangelism with our heavenly Father's longing heart for lost souls is the key to a blessed life of faith that saves the many lost souls around us, and at the same time one is always awake spiritually and overcomes trials and tribulations and always triumphs.

Our Heavenly Father's Aching Heart and Tears

On my way to work this morning, I stopped at a fast-food restaurant in the neighborhood. It was time to go out to the parking lot after planting the powerful seeds of the Gospel with the GO! tracts in several languages, as there were many White people, Black people, and several Latino families. After planting dozens of Gospel seeds, I was coming out to the parking lot. But suddenly, tears of repentance flowed out with a surprising emotion.

Not long ago, I was proud that I was living the life of an evangelist pleasing to the Lord while evangelizing to only a dozen souls throughout the year. I was wasting my time ignoring the additional tens of thousands of people living without hearing the Gospel around me. Then I felt sorry for the Lord, who must have waited anxiously for me to go to the countless dying souls around me. For the past several years, I have been evangelizing only a very small number of souls, and I have always lived with a sense of apology toward the Lord and the burden of working harder for the Lord. However, it was only this morning that I came to understand the heart of the Lord.

"Dear Lord, I have been saying that I love You and serve You, and I have been zealous for the ministry of the church and fellowship with the saints for the past few decades, but I have not been able to go to the lost souls for whom You have been waiting for so long."

"Lord, how sad are You? I repent of the past years of not being able to understand Your pity for the countless dying souls that are scattered everywhere I go. Lord, from now on, until the day when You come, I will testify of the Gospel to countless souls, regardless of time or season." I cried for two years and walked around carrying GO! tracts.

Late at night, lying in bed, driving a car, and even sitting in the office at work, I realized the meaning of endless tears. Those thick tears that flowed endlessly through my heart were the tears shed by my heavenly Father, whom I love so much, who mourns for the dying souls.

As the number of people in whom I planted the seeds of the Gospel surpassed tens of thousands, tears flowed wherever I went. As I continued my journey as a GO! Evangelist, there was a question I always wanted to ask my heavenly Father.

"Heavenly Father, why don't the tears stop flowing while I'm sharing this good news?"

But this GO! Evangelist already knew the answer. Every time I cried the name of Jesus Christ hundreds of times a day, I saw the Lord suffering on the cross. I could see the dear Lord who suffered and took up that cross to atone for our sins. "Lord, let these souls meet You too. Help them to understand deeply in their hearts who God is, how unforgivable sinners are, and why Christ had to come and take up the cross to save them!"

The Lord wept as He looked at the people of the city of Jerusalem who were on the way to destruction, refusing to accept Jesus Christ as their Savior and Lord to the very end.

And when he was come near, he beheld the city, and wept over it. (Luke 19:41)

When Jesus wept, His heavenly Father also wept, and when tears flowed down Jesus' cheeks, tears flowed down the heavenly Father's cheeks. Jesus shed these tears for the people who were to be judged, when He foresaw God's terrible final judgment. These sad tears were also for the people who did not listen to the Gospel of the kingdom.

O Jerusalem, Jerusalem, thou that killest the prophets, and stonest them which are sent unto thee, how often would I have gathered thy children together, even as a hen gathereth her chickens under her wings, and ye would not! (Matthew 23:37)

He wept over the punishment they would receive for their disobedience, namely, destruction. Just as the Lord wept in

Jerusalem in those days, He is angry and weeps at the current church that is not obeying even at this time.

Jehovah's Witnesses are Heretics; Should We Preach to Them Too?

Yes, of course. They, too, are the objects of evangelism that must be saved and go to heaven. The reason they are heretics is because they believe in another Jesus, one different than the Jesus mentioned in the Bible. Ninety-nine percent of Christians say this when Jehovah's Witnesses visit their home to evangelize: "We go to church." And they coldly send them away. Since it is said that one soul is more precious than the world, we should have pity on their souls.

> But sanctify the Lord God in your hearts: and be ready always to give an answer to every man that asketh you a reason of the hope that is in you with meekness and fear. (1 Peter 3:15)

What Do Jehovah's Witnesses Believe?

The heresy known today as Jehovah's Witnesses began in 1870 in Pennsylvania with a Bible study led by Charles Taze Russell.

A close examination of their doctrinal positions on important topics such as the divinity of Jesus, salvation, the Trinity, the Holy Spirit, and redemption reveals that they do not adhere to the orthodox positions of Christianity. Jehovah's Witnesses believe that Jesus is the same as the archangel Michael the warrior. This contradicts many Scriptures that explicitly declare that Jesus is God.

> In the beginning was the Word, and the Word was with God, and the Word was God. (John 1:1)

> And the Word was made flesh, and dwelt among us, (and we beheld his glory, the glory as of the only begotten of the Father,) full of grace and truth. (John 1:14)

> Jesus said unto them, Verily, verily, I say unto you, Before Abraham was, I am. (John 8:58)

> I and my Father are one. (John 10:30)

Jehovah's Witnesses believe that salvation comes through a combination of faith, good works, and obedience.

This contradicts many Scriptures that proclaim salvation by grace through faith.

> For God so loved the world, that he gave his only begotten Son, that whosoever believeth in him should not perish, but have everlasting life. (John 3:16)

> For by grace are ye saved through faith; and that not of yourselves: it is the gift of God: not of works, lest any man should boast. (Ephesians 2:8–9)

> Not by works of righteousness which we have done, but according to his mercy he saved us, by the washing of regeneration, and renewing of the Holy Ghost. (Titus 3:5)

Jehovah's Witnesses deny the Trinity, believing that Jesus is a creature and that the Holy Spirit is essentially a non-life force of God. The Watchtower Bible and Tract Society has changed the text of the Bible to align their Bible with their false doctrine, instead of placing their doctrine on what the Bible actually teaches.

There is probably no religious group more passionate and more faithful than Jehovah's Witnesses in their preaching and missionary work. Unfortunately, their messages are full of distortions, deceptions, and false doctrines. I pray that God will open the blindfolded eyes of Jehovah's Witnesses so that they can see the truth of the Gospel and the intimate teachings of God's Word.

Actual Meeting with Passionate Evangelists of Jehovah's Witnesses

It was a cold Saturday morning in winter. Two evangelists, Jehovah's Witnesses, who visited almost every week, knocked on my door again. We kept silent, believing that if we waited long enough, they would give up and leave, but they waited patiently and knocked on the door.

Suddenly I felt full of pity for them. Since the weather was freezing cold, I thought that they, too, were poor souls who needed to hear the true Gospel and be saved. I opened the front door with the intention of meeting them and talking to them.

They were shivering in the cold, but they greeted me warmly. Two ladies said they wanted to talk about the Bible and asked if they could spare some time. I welcomed them and said that I would like to ask them a few questions before allowing them to enter my house, and if they could answer them correctly, I would welcome them into my house.

First of all, I told them that I am also an evangelist of Jesus Christ, and I teach evangelism seminars at various churches. I said I would like to know if they had been saved and had the confidence and joy that they would go to heaven if God called them even today. The answers provided by the Jehovah's Witnesses were vivid testimony to why they were clearly heretics who must be saved by the true Gospel of Christ.

The kingdom of heaven they believe in is not a place where all Christians enter after death, but only specially chosen ones (144,000 of Jehovah's Witnesses) can enter. The kingdom of God, which will be ruled by Christ forever on earth, will be built on this earth, and this kingdom is the earthly paradise they claim. As Jehovah's Witnesses on earth, they claim to be able to enter the country if they diligently preach about it and do good deeds.

This nation is not a paradise for believers in Jesus, but a paradise for those who are Jehovah's Witnesses. And this kingdom is not a kingdom that is created after being destroyed by fire on this earth, but it is established on this earth and insists on the doctrine that it will continue forever.

I politely explained why I couldn't invite them into my house, and I let them go. On this cold winter day, I sent them with a heart of prayer, asking for mercy so that those souls who are going to hell can be saved by God's grace.

Why Is Mormonism a Cult?

The Church of Jesus Christ of Latter-day Saints are also called Mormons. Mormonism, like Jehovah's Witnesses and Seventh-day Adventists, is a cult that originated in the United States.

Mormons believe that the Bible is the accurately translated Word of God, but they also believe that the Book of Mormon is the Word of God. Their belief in the Book of Mormon as the Word of God in addition to the Bible proves them to be a clear heresy. However, contrary to the preconceived notion of heresy, the outward appearance of their daily life appeared to be wholesome, moral, kind, and friendly. The appearance of the young Mormon missionaries who are doing missionary work in neat clothes and clean looks gives us a good feeling.

Many people are drawn to this attraction and into Mormonism. But here lies the terrifying satanic trap of Mormons. Peeling off the attractive appearance, you can discover that lurking inside the reality are false teachings and terrifying spiritual deception.

First, the Mormon Church teaches that the Bible alone is not enough, so they believe in the Book of Mormon as the Word of God with the same authority as the Bible. Furthermore, Mormons assert that God continues to reveal and refer to the kingdom of God. Mormonism's claim is completely inconsistent with Christianity, which believes only in the Bible as the only rule for salvation and faith life. Mormonism denies the sufficiency and completeness of the Bible.

Second, Mormons deny the deity of Trinity. They claim that God the Father has a body of flesh and bones, which can be seen with the human eye. This claim is completely contrary to the Bible, which clearly teaches that God is spirit and that we cannot see Him.

> God is a Spirit: and they that worship him must worship him in spirit and in truth. (John 4:24)

> Now unto the King eternal, immortal, invisible, the only wise God, be honour and glory for ever and ever. Amen. (1 Timothy 1:17)

> Behold my hands and my feet, that it is I myself: handle me, and see; for a spirit hath not flesh and bones, as ye see me have. (Luke 24:39)

> Who is the image of the invisible God, the firstborn of every creature. (Colossians 1:15)

Jesus is of the same essence as God the Father, and it is clear that Mormonism is a heresy that completely denies the Trinity. Mormonism does not recognize the original sin of humankind due to the sin of Adam; it only admits each person's own sins. Regarding salvation, it is argued that faith in Jesus Christ alone is not sufficient to obtain salvation, and that in addition to faith, an act of obedience must be accompanied. They claim that Jesus does not complete our salvation but only provides an opportunity for salvation. This means that we must obtain salvation by our own strength through the door of salvation that Jesus opened. But the Bible clearly teaches that we can be saved only through faith in Jesus Christ, because Jesus Christ has already accomplished everything for our salvation. The

Mormon view of salvation, which emphasizes human works as a prerequisite for salvation other than faith, is clearly heretical and satanic teaching.

Mormons claim that Mormonism is the only true church that has been restored to the earth and that only Mormons have salvation. The Bible points out that many false prophets will arise and deceive many people as a sign of the last days.

> And many false prophets shall rise, and shall deceive many. (Matthew 24:11)

> Beware of false prophets, which come to you in sheep's clothing, but inwardly they are ravening wolves. (Matthew 7:15)

All of us believers should stand firm in the teachings of the Bible, which is God's only Word of truth, and we should be armed with wisdom, knowledge, and faith to discern false spirits from their teachings.

How Are Mormons Doing Missionary Work?

Young missionaries, married couple missionaries, and regular members carry out this huge missionary program. Young missionaries are usually young people between the ages of 19 and 20 who have graduated from high school or are in their first year or sophomore year of college. Like the seventy disciples at the time of Christ, who were sent out into the world on an evangelistic mission, they travel in pairs and preach sixteen hours a day, six days a week. Passionate young people consider it a great honor to be called as a missionary, so they put off college education or work, and they put off marriage and dedicate themselves to missionary work for two years.

In the past, mostly young Americans were in charge of missionary work, but today, many young people from churches around the world also leave and work as missionaries. General members of the Church of Jesus Christ of Latter-day Saints are also zealous for evangelism. All lay people are encouraged to serve their neighbors as light and salt, striving to set a good example and be zealous. Their deeds and their passion for missionary work are commendable, and many are drawn into Mormonism by this charm, but we believers must realize their false teachings and terrifying spiritual deception and stand firm on the rock of faith.

Great Blessings the Lord Has Prepared for GO! Evangelists

The first blessing is that our evangelists receive the heavenly reward that saves souls that are more precious than the world. God loves us who believe in Jesus Christ and become God's children so much that He wants us to work together with our evangelists who embrace the Father's love for the sake of saving precious souls.

> I have planted, Apollos watered; but God gave the increase. So then neither is he that planteth any thing, neither he that watereth; but God that giveth the increase. Now he that planteth and he that watereth are one: and every man shall receive his own reward according to his own labour. (1 Corinthians 3:6–8)

That is why He wants the saints who live the life of an evangelist with joy to receive the reward prepared for them.

> And they that be wise shall shine as the brightness of the
> firmament; and they that turn many to righteousness
> as the stars for ever and ever. (Daniel 12:3)

God has prepared the blessing formula of evangelism and heavenly blessing, and He is waiting for us to work together.

The second and more important blessing is that whenever GO! Evangelists go out and testify of the Gospel, they can restore and sustain the thrill of salvation. It is the wisdom of God who prepared us to live a life of powerfully proclaiming the cross of Christ with the joy of salvation, that is, thanks to God for saving us and the joy of being saved.

God wants you to keep in your heart like a burning fire the essence of faith, which cannot be endured without proclaiming your passion for the Gospel, like Paul.

> For though I preach the gospel, I have nothing to glory
> of: for necessity is laid upon me; yea, woe is unto me, if
> I preach not the gospel! (1 Corinthians 9:16)

The Gospel that the GO! Evangelists boldly go and cry out to dozens or hundreds of people a day is that we are sinners but that nevertheless, God loved us unconditionally when we were sinners and saved us through His only begotten Son, Jesus Christ.

> But God commendeth his love toward us, in that, while
> we were yet sinners, Christ died for us. (Romans 5:8)

What Is Your Passion Index for the Gospel?

You can determine the measure of your love for the Lord by how powerfully the Gospel, the mystery of the cross of Christ, is being proclaimed in your life. If you look at your passion for the Gospel, you can see how merciful and loving you are for the dying souls around you. If you are a person who personally experienced the crucifixion of Christ, you can't help but hold in your heart God's compassion for lost souls.

The memory of accepting Jesus Christ as my Savior and Lord as a one-time confession of faith in the Lord's crucifixion for my salvation can never be enough to possess the passion of an evangelist with a prophetic mission. If you know the content of the Gospel only with intellectual consent, you will never suffer for the sake of the Gospel. The reason why so many church members do not experience the thrill of salvation is because they do not realize how poor and wretched sinners are, and they live without even imagining how frightening and terrible God's final judgment is as it slowly approaches for unforgiven sinners.

As soon as the early church members experienced the Holy Spirit on the day of Pentecost, the contents of the Gospel began to burn like a fire in their hearts, and they were compelled to boldly preach the Gospel of the cross by giving their lives to the world. These were the people of the cross who gave up everything in the world for the harvest of souls. They did not care about the suffering and persecution that came to them for the glory of Christ, and they willingly followed the Lord for the reward of heaven and the glory of that day.

But God forbid that I should glory, save in the cross of our Lord Jesus Christ, by whom the world is crucified unto me, and I unto the world. (Galatians 6:14)

As the number of people I met in the field of the Gospel increased, quite a few people were apathetic and some even showed a hostile reaction. One adversary I met the other day shouted that he had absolutely no intention of going to heaven. As the number of adversaries increased, the words I meditate on gave me strength to assure me that the Holy Spirit was always right by my side and always with me.

We then, as workers together with him, beseech you also that ye receive not the grace of God in vain. (For he saith, I have heard thee in a time accepted, and in the day of salvation have I succoured thee: behold, now is the accepted time; behold, now is the day of salvation.) (2 Corinthians 6:1–2)

I meditate on these words: "This evangelist, who is standing in front of you right now to testify to the Gospel of salvation, is not an ordinary person but a worker who is greatly used by the God of power who created all things in the universe and operates through the Word. Since this is a golden opportunity only possible by God's grace, accept that grace today and be saved before it's too late."

Whenever I meditated on these words, no matter what situation I encountered, I was always confident, and as soon as it was revealed that the target of evangelism was someone who had not yet been saved, I looked at the person with the compassion and sorrow of the Lord with tears in my eyes. Then I was able to boldly testify of the Gospel through the GO! Gospel tracts. However, in proportion to the number of people who received GO! tracts, seeds of the Gospel, even more enemies were waiting for me. Some adversaries would be very cynical and would say, "I am not going to heaven, but there is a special place I will go with lots of my friends."

Whenever I lead evangelism seminars in numerous churches in the United States, I ask the members the following questions. "What percentage of regenerated Christians do you think you will find if you evangelize one hundred people you meet on the streets of America, which is known as a Christian country?" The answer to this question is usually, "From 50 to 90 percent." Some people ask, "How do you know if the person you are evangelizing is a born-again Christian?" However, a born-again Christian cannot hide his identity with moderation.

God's people, whose spirit is alive, respond immediately with a welcome and bright smile. "I am a born-again Christian too. God bless you!" Of course, the reality of the United States, a Christian country where the answer "From 80 to 90 percent" should be correct, is seriously pessimistic. In the meantime, while evangelizing to Americans on the streets, along with the saints who have completed evangelism seminars in various cities in the United States, as well as in meeting more than fifty thousand people whom I personally met and witnessed the Gospel to over the past few years, there were only 2 to 3 percent who were saved.

In addition, the sad and surprising reality is that although I was looking forward to evangelism on the streets and in shopping malls in many cities, there were many evangelical churches around, but there were hardly any evangelists of Americans or other ethnic groups.

Church members all over the United States order GO! Gospel tracts from hundreds to thousands of copies.

Even this morning, as soon as I entered the GO! Evangelism Ministry office, I reviewed the numbers of tracts ordered online by numerous churches and individual GO! Evangelists across the country, and I can't tell you how thrilled and excited I was at the prompt delivery requests of over ten thousand tracts in various languages. Hours after I shipped all our tract orders, I could still hear my heart beating rapidly with amazement and joy.

One church in Texas is undergoing a spiritual awakened and being revitalized due to many GO! Evangelists living the life of a passionate evangelist over the past few years. This time, they ordered an additional five thousand tracts.

A church that evangelizes thousands of commuters every month on the New York subways is making history by planting the seeds of the Gospel in nearly eighty thousand souls by dozens of evangelism team members over the past few months.

With continued enthusiasm, they ordered an additional four thousand tracts in bilingual, English, Spanish, and Chinese. Every time I hear the numerous testimonies from the members who evangelize passionately, I am just moved and grateful. The church in Los Angeles also orders thousands of tracts again and again. For the past several months, dozens of GO! Evangelists have gone downtown every Saturday to areas with large Black populations, and to the east, where there are many Latinos, and the amazing testimony that they have planted the seeds of the Gospel in more than seventy-thousand souls continues.

The number of members who order tracts through the following websites, personally and through their church, is increasing across the country in the United States.

www.GospelTracts.org

www.BibleTracts.org

The GO! Evangelists who have personally experienced our heavenly Father's tears and joy that He gives to the evangelists know very well the Lord's heartfelt desire to go to the field of the Gospel together. "Would you like to go with Me to the place where countless lost souls are waiting for us today?" Whenever I hear the Lord's voice, I load the evangelism bag full of tracts into the car with joy and emotion and run to the field of the Gospel with the Lord today.

Another Miracle in Houston, Texas

A small church of thirty families in Houston recently started a new outreach ministry where their youth members visit at least one thousand homes every month, planting seeds of the Gospel, fully utilizing GO! Gospel tracts. It is their desire to evangelize all the homes in the Houston area. All GO! Evangelists pray for the blessing that countless souls in the Houston area will return to the Lord because of all the young evangelists of the church who diligently plant the seeds of the Gospel.

Today, Houston is Texas's most populous city and the fourth-largest city in the U.S. Its 2.3 million citizens are spread among the city and Harris County, with a density of 3,663 people per square mile. At 600 square miles, Houston's land area is actually considerably larger than the city of Los Angeles, and at 3,663 residents per square mile, its population density is even lower.

We pray that all believers in many other cities in the U.S. will also rise up and start planting the seeds of the Gospel to countless perishing souls, as His coming is imminent.

An Urgent Call from a Pastor of the Church in the Mid-East Region of the U.S.

It was January 12, 2010, the morning of a major earthquake in Haiti, and all the news media was reporting the disaster. A pastor of a church urgently called our GO! Evangelism Ministry office. The pastor said that ten thousand tracts in the Haitian language were urgently needed because a mission team of ten people from the church was being urgently dispatched to Haiti.

When a 7.0 magnitude major earthquake struck Haiti, it left its capital, Port-au-Prince, devastated. About 220,000 people were reportedly killed; among them were 102 United Nations staff who lost their lives when the building housing the mission there, known as MINUSTAH, collapsed. I told the pastor that our ministry did not have tracts printed in Haitian language yet. "But how did you know, Pastor, to call our office?" I asked.

The pastor said that he hastily searched for Haitian language tracts online, but he could not find them anywhere. He called the Billy Graham Association, thinking they would definitely have Haitian tracts. So he called them and asked them to provide at least ten thousand Haitian tracts. But their answer was very disappointing. The Billy Graham Association replied, "We don't have the tract, but we know a tract ministry in California that should have the Haitian tracts." "They told me to call GO! Evangelism Ministry office, and they gave me the phone number of this ministry office," the pastor said.

Unfortunately we couldn't supply the Haitian language tracts immediately, but from that day on, our ministry started working on the translation immediately. A few months later, the Haitian tracts were printed, and within six months, many churches and missionary agencies ordered the Haitian tracts. Within a year, we had more than 100,000 copies shipped. Thanks be to the Lord that the Haitian language tract has become one of the most-ordered tract so far.

Our Heavenly Father's Burning Heart, *Splagchnizomai*

In Matthew 9:36, Jesus said that He had compassion on the multitude of people who were wandering, not knowing the Father and not knowing where to go. In English, *compassion* is a compound word; "com" means "together," and "passion" means "to feel extreme pain." The movie *The Passion of the Christ* depicts the excruciating pain that Jesus felt when He was beaten and His flesh was torn and He carried that heavy cross.

The Greek word for *compassion*, *splagchnizomai*, literally means to be moved so deeply by something that you feel it in the pit of your stomach. This word expresses the heart of the Father and is used twelve times in the Gospels. The Greeks use this word to express the heartbreak of the Lord, who loves all human beings and wants to be saved, as "the pain of twisting all the internal organs." That is, if you want to live the life of a passionate and persistent evangelist who goes and testifies the Gospel to save the countless perishing souls who are on the path of eternal destruction, you must have such a love of the Lord as if all your internal organs were twisted. An evangelist who has such extreme pain for lost souls cannot endure without going to the countless children of God who are wandering outside the church, those who cannot but go to hell if they are not saved today.

True Freedom and Abundant Blessings Given to Evangelists

It is only now that this evangelist can walk with God the Father in the truth, just as He said, "The truth will set you free." After experiencing the heartbreaking tears of my heavenly Father and the joy of the Father toward the evangelist who testifies of the Gospel, I learned the thrill of walking with Him moment by moment. It is now that I clearly understand why I have to exist in this world. It is only now that I am free to continue in close association with my perfect Father. Jesus Christ is the real truth and power; Christ who now lives in me has given me true freedom.

Then said Jesus unto his disciples, If any man will come after me, let him deny himself, and take up his cross, and follow me. (Matthew 16:24)

The Gospel cannot be preached without the sacrifice of the evangelist. In fact, there is no royal road to evangelism. Evangelism is very simple: you hear the Lord's voice saying, "Go and proclaim!" and then you obey and spend your time and money to go and proclaim it. The most important thing when going to evangelize is to pray for the many souls you will meet today. We do not know their name or race or nationality, but when we obey and preach the good news of salvation like the prophet Jonah, then the Holy Spirit, who is the subject of evangelism, moves their hearts and saves them.

> And when the Gentiles heard this, they were glad, and glorified the word of the Lord: and as many as were ordained to eternal life believed. (Acts 13:48)

The serious problem of today's churches is that they prefer social events and fellowship rather than shedding tears for lost souls, denying their own worldly comforts and desires to bear witness to the Gospel, and bearing their share of the cross. We are living in an age of profound spiritual confusion and ignorance, in which it is difficult to find believers who are interested in the heart of the Lord who mourned and wept for Jerusalem. They all are focused only on believing in Jesus and receiving blessings. The Lord weeps over the church at this time, which is tainted with secularism, is not interested in the heavenly Father's heartfelt feelings for lost souls, and is ignoring the Day of Judgment that is soon to come. If we understand the Lord's tears even a little, we should go to the countless dying souls around us with the same heart as Jesus. We, the GO! Evangelists, must let the tears of Jesus, the tears of our heavenly Father, flow from our hearts.

My Firm Determination to Live the Next Two Years as a Devoted GO! Evangelist!

The greatest joy, happiness, and glory that believers enjoy is to share in the joy of the heavenly Father. But why are so many saints unable to enjoy this joy and blessing?

It is because we do not know what God is most pleased with and values the most, so we cannot be satisfied with God and cannot participate in God's joy.

As I was beginning to experience this great joy while planting seeds of the Gospel, I decided to set aside the next two years as a period of total devotion in order to plant the seeds of the Gospel to as many perishing souls as possible. My initial plan was to plant the seeds of the Gospel to at least four or five hundred people every week. This decision and plan started fifteen years ago and continued for two years, and the grace of God I experienced during those years was truly a wonderful and grateful blessing.

The evangelism that started on the street planted the seeds of the Gospel in almost five hundred people every week, including many fast-food restaurants, shopping malls, and Jobber Wholesale Market in downtown Los Angeles. Everywhere I went, it was crowded with people, and most of the people welcomed the GO! tracts in English, Spanish, and bilingual.

I have planted the seeds of the Gospel in over fifty thousand souls over those two years, and every time I planted the seeds, the prayer I offered to the Lord was this: "Lord, I have planted the seeds of the Gospel to many perishing souls. Please move these lost souls by the inspiration of the Holy Spirit and save them."

The grace and blessings of God that I experienced for the first year could not be expressed in words.

The greatest grace that I experienced was that my heart, which was very dry, changed into a watered garden, and tears overflowed in my eyes.

At this moment, I fully understood why the apostle Paul said in 1 Corinthians 9:16, "Woe is unto me, if I preach not the gospel!" The greatest and most amazing blessing that all believers can enjoy is to live a life of faith filled with love in a relationship with the Lord. Even though I was working hard in my life of faith, I always felt a sense of pressure from not being able to give more love to the Lord. Now I clearly understand why Paul said, "Woe is unto me." I clearly understood the words of woe while witnessing the Gospel to countless lost souls.

The Burden of My Heartache Totally Lifted

As I began to bear witness to the Gospel to many perishing souls, the burden of my heartache and the burden of apologizing to the Lord was totally lifted. And my heart began to fill with joy, passion, and ecstasy. Oh, that was it! It was the realization that this was the joy the Lord had been waiting for. The Lord allowed me the joy and gratitude that I had never experienced during my decades of church life. It was only now that I began to feel our heavenly Father's pity for the lost souls.

While sowing the seeds of the Gospel from thousands to tens of thousands, the meaning of the tears that constantly flowed in my heart was the pity that so few were saved.

At the same time, the number of those who opposed the Gospel was increasing. This was not my only regret. There were many churches around where I evangelized, but it was a sad reality that I had hardly ever seen churches that actively evangelized.

By the grace of God, I was able to end my two years as an evangelist when I made a vow to God with joy and gratitude as my passion for the Gospel witness grew hotter.

God urged me to write this evangelism book, *America, Repent and Believe the Gospel*, with the determination to raise up thousands of believers across the country as active and enthusiastic GO! Evangelists and to send them to the front line of the Gospel. In this way, they can bear more abundant fruits of the Gospel with this precious and wonderful grace, wisdom, and greater passion that the Lord has allowed me to experience for two solid years.

The Lord reminds all GO! Evangelists of the following Scriptures once again to effectively plant the seeds of the Gospel with joy and boldness.

Three passages urge all GO! Evangelists to go out and plant the seeds of the Gospel to as many perishing souls as possible, totally relying upon the power of the Holy Spirit.

1. "And my speech and my preaching was not with enticing words of man's wisdom, but in demonstration of the Spirit and of power" (1 Corinthians 2:4).

The chance of witnessing the Gospel that God has prepared for this evangelist is a very important opportunity that is always full of fear and trembling. When this message is delivered through a tract, it is also a proclamation of the Word of God. Although the tract is delivered momentarily, all evangelists must first pray so that the inspiration and power of the Holy Spirit may be revealed to all who receive this tract.

I sincerely hope that all the saints who deliver the Word of God, including myself, have the same heart as the apostle Paul. Planting the seeds of the Gospel in dozens or hundreds of souls every day is like giving countless number of souls the last chance to be saved. We must pray that at least one soul a day may return to the Lord.

There are a lot of really good talkers in this world. There are people who say what they are trying to convey in a logical and straightforward manner, and there are people who make people laugh with their humor and wit, and then, after a while, they bring tears from the eyes of the listeners with a moving story. There are people who are so good at speaking that others say, "He speaks well, in such a moving way." This is a talent that many people envy. However, the apostle Paul says that he did not rely on such learned speech or wisdom when witnessing to the Gospel in the Corinthian church. Paul was concerned that if he preached the Gospel with flashy speech, then the Gospel, the most important thing, would be obscured. So when Paul preached the Gospel in the church in Corinth, he did not rely on human wisdom but only preached the word of the cross.

> For I determined not to know anything among you, save Jesus Christ, and him crucified. (1 Corinthians 2:2)

The apostle Paul focused on only one message that the world did not know or possess: that Jesus Christ was crucified and died for sinners. Paul was not afraid of tribulation because of the Gospel. Paul never feared dying while preaching the Gospel. Then why did Paul say that he was weak in heart, fearful, and very trembling while he was in Corinth?

Paul was afraid that he would not be able to fully carry out the mission of preaching the Gospel entrusted to him by God because he was a very small and weak person who preached this Gospel, compared to the value of the Gospel of which he was in charge. Paul could sweeten people's ears with his oratory and persuasive words whenever he wanted. But Paul never used the worldly wisdom to deceive the crowds like this. He confessed that he relied entirely on the manifestation and power of the Holy Spirit.

Through this, Paul is teaching us that the salvation of a person is not based on human wisdom, but is entirely through the testimony of the Holy Spirit, which is the power of God. Dear GO! Evangelists, like the confession of the apostle Paul, our evangelists are not relying on their own human eloquence and excellent discourse, but they only reveal the cross of Christ and plant the seeds of the whole Gospel, completely depending on the power of the Holy Spirit. I sincerely hope all of you become faithful and powerful GO! Evangelists.

2. "I have planted, Apollos watered; but God gave the increase. So then neither is he that planteth any thing, neither he that watereth; but God that giveth the increase. Now he that planteth and he that watereth are one: and every man shall receive his own reward according to his own labour" (1 Corinthians 3:6–8).

First of all, we evangelists know well that God is omnipotent and lacks nothing. God reveals to us His name in Exodus 3:14: He is the God who said. "I AM THAT I AM." God Himself is the first and the last; He exists, and He is perfect in every way. God is the Almighty, perfect in Himself, who does not need any human service or help.

In 1 Corinthians 3:7, it says, "So then neither is he that planteth any thing, neither he that watereth; but God that giveth the increase." No matter how hard a person perspires, plants, waters, and toils for God, only God makes the seeds grow. Even if a farmer plows, sows, and waters a field, he will not reap any fruit without the work of God, who rules all nature.

God Wants to Work with GO! Evangelists

God is all-powerful and perfect. The Bible clearly shows that God is self-sufficient in all things and does not need anything from man. But at the same time, the Bible also clearly shows that God works with man. In 1 Corinthians 3:9, it says, "We are labourers together with God." The Bible shows that God does not need people to work, but at the same time He wants to work with people. These two facts seem to contradict each other, but they are not; in fact, they are in harmony with each other. Obviously, God is perfect in Himself and does not require human help, but the principle that God works on this earth is that He always works through people.

Why does God want to work through people? To give our evangelists a reward in heaven!

Why does God want to work with us? If God can do it all, why is He calling us? Wouldn't it be a thousand times more effective to send angels to preach the Gospel to people? The reason almighty God has called us today and wants to work with us is not to ask for anything from us but to reward us according to our small efforts. God can do all things alone without us, but He called us, foolish and very weak though we are, in order to work with us and reward us. God has given us breath and life, and above all, He has saved us by giving His life. He poured out on us an unbearable love that cannot be put to measure and whose price cannot be measured simply because we have believed in Him without any conditions. And now He wants to give us a mission, engage us, and reward us through it.

3. "For though I preach the gospel, I have nothing to glory of: for necessity is laid upon me; yea, woe is unto me, if I preach not the gospel! For if I do this thing willingly, I have a reward: but if against my will, a dispensation of the gospel is committed unto me" (1 Corinthians 9:16–17).

The Holy Spirit is the Spirit that makes us believe in Jesus Christ. The Holy Spirit is at work in anyone who believes in Jesus. That's why 1 Corinthians 12:3 says, "No man can say that Jesus is the Lord, but by the Holy Ghost." In other words, we believe in Jesus as our Savior through the Holy Spirit. In John 6:39, we can see that God's chosen people will not be lost by a single one, and all will be saved without exception. God is pleased to save those who believe in Jesus through our evangelism, even though God has made a plan of salvation and fulfilled it 100 percent as it is. In 1 Corinthians 1:21, it says, "For after that in the wisdom of God the world by wisdom knew not God, it pleased God by the foolishness of preaching to save them that believe."

We humans have lost the wisdom and ability to know God because of our sins. Therefore, no one can know and trust God by himself. But when we go out to evangelize, there are people who receive the evangelism and believe in Jesus. God was pleased to save those who received evangelism and believed in Jesus. Who are the people you trust at this time? They are the people God has ordained to give us eternal life. That's why Acts13:48 says, "And when the Gentiles heard this, they were glad, and glorified the word of the Lord: and as many as were ordained to eternal life believed." When we evangelize, all those whom God decided before the foundation of the world to live with Him and give them eternal life will all believe.

Therefore, when our evangelists planted the seeds of the Gospel and many perishing souls were saved, we also labored by giving our time, material, and body, but they are God's chosen people, and the Holy Spirit worked to save these souls. We should give thanks and praise to the Lord. God made this plan of salvation and fulfilled it as it is, but in spite of this, Jesus told us to go into all the world and preach the Gospel to every creature (Mark 16:15). This is the Great Commission given to all the saints. This is not a condition of our choice, but it is our mission that we must obey with joy and boldness, which we must obey at the risk of our lives.

Why did Jesus give us the mission to plant the seeds of the Gospel?

1. When our saints are zealous for evangelism, our faith can lead a healthy life filled with joy, gratitude, and passion. A church that evangelizes with zeal is healthy and growing rapidly. However, even if you believe in Jesus for the rest of your life, if you do not have the passion for the Gospel and the fruits of salvation, you are not a healthy believer. We do not know how important it is to have the fruit of salvation through us. Those who do not evangelize and do not have the fruit of salvation must repent because they do not obey the Lord's great command. Jesus cursed the fig tree, which had no fruit and had only leaves. Then the roots dried up and died. This is a warning to us. From the outside, it seems that only the leaves are thick and they believe in Jesus, but it is a curse to have no fruit of salvation.

2. Jesus gave us the mission to preach the Gospel because if we do not preach the Gospel, we will be woeful. Because preaching the Gospel is the Lord's great command, it is something everyone should do, and it is absolutely not something to boast about when we have done it. This is our mission, which we must do even if we do not want to. The Bible clearly indicates that if we do not preach the Gospel, we will be woeful.

3. Jesus gave us the mission to preach the Gospel so that we can taste and live the kingdom of heaven on earth. Why do we receive God's love and blessings like this if we live the life of an evangelist for the sake of the Lord and the Gospel? It is because we share in what God is very pleased with. That is why the evangelist will always serve the Lord and receive the Lord's love and blessings while enjoying the heavenly life on this earth.

4. Jesus gave us the mission to preach the Gospel in order to reward us in the future. Revelation 2:10 says, "Be thou faithful unto death, and I will give thee a crown of life." Revelation 22:12 says, "Behold, I come quickly; and my reward is with me, to give every man according as his work shall be." The Bible strongly emphasizes that if we are faithful for the Lord and the Gospel, God will surely reward us. The rewards we receive in this world are temporary, but the rewards we receive in heaven are eternal joy and glory. There are people who say they believe in Jesus but do not evangelize, do not do service, and do not want to work even a little.

People who simply and easily believe in Jesus and then go to heaven are not wise people. In the future, when you stand before the Lord, you will not receive any reward and will be forever ashamed and full of regret.

A faithful disciple of the Lord follows the path of the Lord. A disciple of the Lord is a person who takes up his cross and bears all sufferings for the salvation of souls. Believers who experience grace will surely live the life of an evangelist.

And, behold, I come quickly; and my reward is with me, to give every man according as his work shall be. (Revelation 22:12)

Chapter 9: Stand Strong and Firm in Your Faith

Examine and Reconfirm Your Faith

Lord, help us to stand strong and firm in our faith as joyful and enthusiastic evangelists planting the powerful seeds of the Gospel.

I have felt the heart of the Lord while giving evangelism seminar meetings in numerous churches throughout the nation. Too many church members are satisfied with false salvation. The important thing in the life of faith is that we must first check whether we are truly saved and then live a born-again Christian life. Many Christians are living spiritually asleep without enthusiasm for sowing the seeds of the Gospel that the Lord earnestly asks for.

If you are a believer living a life that pleases the Lord, the following confession by the apostle Paul will give you a fervent challenge and new determination in your heart:

> But none of these things move me, neither count I my life dear unto myself, so that I might finish my course with joy, and the ministry, which I have received of the Lord Jesus, to testify the gospel of the grace of God. (Acts 20:24)

Salvation is the most important, pressing, and urgent thing for all who live in this world.

Salvation means to be saved from sin and to go to heaven and be praised and rewarded as a "good and faithful servant" before the judgment seat of Christ.

The Lord tells us to confirm that we are all surely saved and are living as children of God, that our names are clearly written in the book of life, and that we are believers that God approves and pleases.

> Examine yourselves, whether ye be in the faith; prove your own selves. Know ye not your own selves, how that Jesus Christ is in you, except ye be reprobates? (2 Corinthians 13:5)

If a believer does not have such assurance and confidence, God says firmly that this person is an outcast, unsaved, who has no choice but to go to hell if he leaves this world today.

The Lord clearly shows us who enters the kingdom of heaven and who cannot enter it, including the church members who cannot.

First, let's look at the background of this verse: when Jesus first began His public ministry, after being baptized by John the Baptist, He was led by the Holy Spirit to be tempted by Satan in the wilderness. The Lord who overcame the temptation of Satan was now preaching the Gospel of the kingdom of God.

> From that time Jesus began to preach, and to say, Repent: for the kingdom of heaven is at hand. (Matthew 4:17)

Jesus called His disciples, saying, "Follow me, and I will make you fishers of men" (Matthew 4:19).

He healed many sick, afflicted, and demon-possessed people.

Through His amazing ministry, word of Jesus spread throughout the land, and when Jesus preached the Gospel of the kingdom, thousands of people came to Jesus from Galilee and the southern regions of the Decapolis, Jerusalem, Judea, and across the Jordan River.

The scene in which thousands of people cheering and following Jesus after being healed went up to the mountain to receive Jesus' teachings is the well-known Sermon on the Mount, from Matthew chapters 5–7.

The content of this Sermon on the Mount is, in a word, about the Gospel of the kingdom. Jesus was saying, "The gates of heaven are open to anyone who asks, seeks, or knocks." It was the word of the Gospel that gives the hope of heaven to anyone.

The Most Frightening and Dreadful Words of the Lord

But today, the Lord speaks the most frightening and dreadful words to all who attend church, including in the Old and New Testaments.

> Not everyone that saith unto me, Lord, Lord, shall enter into the kingdom of heaven; but he that doeth the will of my Father which is in heaven. (Matthew 7:21)

Those Church Members Who Cannot Enter the Kingdom of Heaven

Thousands of churchgoers have learned and know that if they accept that Jesus forgave all of their sins on the cross, then they are saved. But today, the Lord is saying that it is very shocking that there are a lot of church members who cannot enter the kingdom of heaven even if they know and confess that the Lord is God.

Then who are the saints who are truly saved and will enter the kingdom of heaven? Jesus says in Matthew 7:21, "He that doeth the will of my Father which is in heaven." Jesus is talking about a person who has established a personal, close, and loving relationship with God and one who obeys the Word of God.

He says that those who are truly saved do not stop with an intellectual assent to know who Jesus is. He says that those who are truly saved are believers who bear abundant fruit that the Lord is very pleased with in a close, beautiful, and loving relationship with God.

> Many will say to me in that day, Lord, Lord, have we not prophesied in thy name? and in thy name have cast out devils? and in thy name done many wonderful works? (Matthew 7:22)

The countless deceased who are not saved on that Day of Judgment will try to persuade the Lord to prove that they are clearly saved before God. Those who say, "Lord, Lord," here are faithful servants who act as prophets, exercise the power to cast out demons, and exercise power in the name of the Lord, so outwardly they can be evaluated as servants of great faith and power.

But even about servants of this kind of power, Jesus says firmly that if they do not do "the will of my Father which is in heaven," they can become those who practice iniquity and will never enter the kingdom of heaven.

The Day of Judgment

Even on the Day of Judgment, the Lord says, "Then will I profess unto them, I never knew you: depart from me, ye that work iniquity" (Matthew 7:23).

They not only knew and confessed that Jesus was God, but they also did amazing work, such as casting out demons and healing the sick in the name of the Lord.

If someone exercised the power to cast out demons and raise the sick at this time, wouldn't you think that he would naturally be saved and go to heaven? He would have lived a life of faith by attending church diligently and attending various meetings and disciple-training seminars without exception, responding with "Amen, amen" to the words proclaimed and confessing that Jesus is Lord, but without a close, loving relationship with Jesus.

But the Lord speaks firmly: "I never knew you; get away from Me!"

Then what is the fundamental problem of the faith of the unsaved church members? What was their religious life, and why would you speak so coldly and heartlessly? Jesus referred to them as "ye that work iniquity." That is, they were lawless, people who lived by sin. Those who lived according to the desires of sin in the center of their hearts, on the throne of their hearts, were those who lived according to their own will. They have the illusion that they are doing something very important in the name of the Lord.

They knew that the Lord was the Son of God, and they called God Father, but they had absolutely no personal, close, and loving relationship with the Lord. As a sure proof of that, it was never a life that pleased the Lord by obeying the Lord's Word. The Lord said they were sinners who work iniquity.

Do You Have Solid Evidence That You Have Been Saved?

If you are not a member of the church and have never heard the Gospel at all, you may feel less injustice. However, if you have been attending church for a long time, but there is no solid evidence that you have been saved 100 percent in your life, if you do not have a passionate, loving, and close relationship with Jesus Christ, Jesus calls such people lawless people. You will fall into hell where eternal despair and suffering continue.

What kind of person is a believer who truly enters the kingdom of heaven with joy and confidence? In chapter 3 of his Gospel, John tells the story of Nicodemus, who was recognized by the apostle John and by the Lord as a sincere and faithful leader of the Jews, and he was also recognized in front of the people.

Nicodemus was a truly outstanding Jewish leader, both personally and spiritually, a Pharisee, a member of the Sanhedrin who was also recognized politically, which would be like a member of Parliament today, and a faithful servant who struggled to live well before God at that time.

He was a leader of the people who were religiously and ethically perfect and pure, and he had tried to keep the law.

Already in the Old Testament, in Ezekiel 36:25–27, God promises to wash away all our sins with clean water, so the grace of forgiveness and the Holy Spirit would be present in that person. The Lord explained in great detail that if this miracle happened, that person was born again. But Nicodemus was still not sure about the matter of eternal life.

Nicodemus came to the Lord with insatiable longing and thirst in his soul, and the most important thing in this longing and thirst was the shocking fact that he had not yet been born again. The Lord and John pointed out that he was recognized as the leader of a people who was religiously and ethically perfect and clean, but at the same time he was not born again.

The Lord said to him, "Art thou a master of Israel, and knowest not these things?" (verse 10). In verse 3, He said, "Except a man be born again, he cannot see the kingdom of God." In verse 5, He said, "Except a man be born of water and of the Spirit, he cannot enter into the kingdom of God."

Are You 100 Percent Sure That You Are Born Again?

Are you certain that you are living as a believer of whom the Lord approves and with whom He is pleased?

Have you really been born again of water and the Holy Spirit? At this time, the Lord is asking each and every one of us the same question: "Have you been truly born again as you've been attending church diligently for a long time and serving faithfully?"

The reason the Lord asks is that you may live as a religiously and ethically clean person, but He says that you have not yet been born again. The Lord is seeing at this time that there is a longing and thirst for eternal life in your heart.

If each one of you stood before the Lord and was judged at the moment when He said, "I never knew you; get away from Me," how terrified and fearful would you be?

How would you react in this desperate situation?

In this moment of absolute desperation, it is the moment that decides whether your soul goes to eternal heaven or eternal hell. You have to be really serious at this crucial moment. You must seize this last chance that the Lord is giving you at this very moment, before you despair at the judgment of the Lord.

Lord, Please Give Me One More Chance!

On that day, many people who were not saved will cry out before the Lord. If at this time today, with the inspiration of the Holy Spirit, you have the true realization and regret that you are a sinner who has not been saved, you must respond with a humble heart and with fear and trembling. You must truly come before the Lord with a sincere heart of repentance and contrition.

The most urgent and important thing at this time is to start a close, personal, and loving relationship with the Lord, which He acknowledges and delights in.

The quickest way is to first know what pleases the Lord the most and what the Lord grieves for the most.

How Much Do You Understand the Heart of Our Lord?

Dear brothers and sisters, how much do you understand the heart of our Lord?

Do you understand that the most pleasing thing to the Lord is the salvation of perishing souls? If you have truly understood God's heart, the grace God has prepared for us now is faith and obedience to overcome in order to witness the Gospel.

Numerous members of the church are working hard to live a life of faith as the people of heaven who possess the certainty of being born again. Even though so many members of the church are struggling like Nicodemus during their years of living of faith for years or decades, there are still many believers who in their hearts are unable to settle the problem of eternal salvation.

The more the members of all churches experience God's great grace, the first thing they want to do is to testify of the Gospel. Why? Because it is the very heart of the Lord. However, perhaps after making the decision to live the life of an evangelist who testifies to the Gospel, they tried several times, but they experienced that evangelism was extremely difficult, burdensome, and fearsome. In that case, the reality is that they are living the life of a lukewarm church member.

However, GO! Gospel tracts, the powerful seeds of the Gospel, are the wisdom and blessing of God who willingly solved this very hard and difficult problem for all of us in one moment. The great blessings of this age given to our Christians are the blessings that can spread the Gospel to all people.

God wants us to rise up and plant the seeds of the Gospel to the millions of souls of more than 300 million people in the country, including nearly 90 million immigrants living in the United States from over 230 countries around the world.

The age we live in now is not an age in which we have ample time to do personal evangelism and relational evangelism, to testify of the Gospel by using the verses recited with our wisdom and persuasive power to the countless perishing souls we meet.

> And my speech and my preaching was not with enticing words of man's wisdom, but in demonstration of the Spirit and of power: that your faith should not stand in the wisdom of men, but in the power of God. (1 Corinthians 2:4–5)

The Sure Way to Know That You Are Unquestionably Saved

In order to be able to 100 percent confirm that the Lord is very pleased with my faith, please read the following words slowly and deeply.

> Blessed are ye, when men shall revile you, and persecute you, and shall say all manner of evil against you falsely, for my sake. Rejoice, and be exceeding glad: for great is your reward in heaven: for so persecuted they the prophets which were before you. (Matthew 5:11–12)

> Blessed are ye, when men shall hate you, and when they shall separate you from their company, and shall reproach you, and cast out your name as evil, for the Son of man's sake. Rejoice ye in that day, and leap for

joy: for, behold, your reward is great in heaven: for in the like manner did their fathers unto the prophets. (Luke 6:22–23)

Why does the world use all means to criticize, hate, and persecute the church? We know that the history of Christianity has been one of suffering and persecution, stained with the blood of martyrdom from the early church established through the twelve apostles after the Pentecost to the present day.

Even at this moment, in many parts of the world, there are countless saints who are being martyred for their faith in Jesus. Why does the world hate and persecute Christianity while not hating other religions?

The above two Bible passages clearly state the reason. It is because the Lord has chosen us to be His own heavenly people. The reason the world persecutes the church and, moreover, persecutes and hates the evangelists who preach the Gospel of the life of Christ is because only Jesus is the truth. The truth of this world is only Jesus Christ.

That is why Satan persecutes and attacks the evangelists who believe in this truth and endure all kinds of hardships to preach.

Are you experiencing difficulties and persecution from the world while you are witnessing the Gospel? In the midst of this, are you longing for the reward you will receive in your hearts before the judgment seat of the Lord?

I congratulate you as a believer who already possesses the joy of heaven that the world cannot bear. Keep your faith until the day you stand before the Lord, and keep planting the seeds of the Gospel with passion for the many lost souls around us. Our Lord and the angels of heaven are cheering you on and waiting for that glorious day.

Living in the Worst Era of Spiritual Invasion

We are living in the worst era of spiritual invasion, in which it is almost impossible to meet a single saved person even if we evangelize to hundreds of people all day.

The most effective evangelism in this age, when so many souls are running toward hell, is to plant the powerful seeds of the Gospel with a smile for every soul we meet, relying 100 percent in God's almighty sovereignty and power of salvation (1 Corinthians 3:6–8).

The core of the Gospel message contained in the GO! tracts is the powerful seed of the Gospel. The easiest and most powerful evangelism method for everyone you meet is as follows.

Hand out GO! tracts, the seeds of eternal life, with a sincere and pleasant smile, and say, "Hi, I have good news for you!" If they ask, "What is it about?" then tell them the truth: "It is a Gospel tract. It will show you how to get to heaven."

God has prepared the following infinite blessings for the saints who actively evangelize in this way.

1. Your faith will grow exponentially with the Holy Spirit as your co-worker (1 Corinthians 2:4–5).

2. You will continue to have the Lord's longing heart for the lost souls.

3. You will be transformed into a passionate believer who thirsts for God's Word and longs for greater grace.

4. You will be able to witness the Gospel with joy and boldness to many perishing souls around you in all ethnic groups. As the Lord said in 2 Timothy 1:8, "Be not thou therefore ashamed of the testimony of our Lord, nor of me his prisoner: but be thou partaker of the afflictions of the gospel according to the power of God." You will become a mature believer who rejoices in suffering along with the Gospel.

In order to become believers who suffer along with the Gospel and who do the Father's will, what we need at this time is to establish a close and personal loving relationship with Jesus.

This is the final conclusion of today's message. Who is a believer who overcomes head-on and wins?

1. Believers who have won the final victory are saints whose names are written in the book of life.

2. After entering the kingdom of heaven, GO! Evangelists will be praised by the Lord as a good and faithful servant at the judgment seat of Christ and receive the reward prepared by the Lord.

For we must all appear before the judgment seat of Christ; that every one may receive the things done in his body, according to that he hath done, whether it be good or bad. (2 Corinthians 5:10)

Examine and Reconfirm Your Faith and Determine Where You Stand

The following represents what this writer has been experiencing while giving evangelism training lectures in hundreds of churches across the country for the past twenty years.

Important Questions

The following two questions were asked to everyone who participated the GO! Evangelism training lectures during many years of my teaching.

1. Have you reached the point in your spiritual life where you know for certain that if you were to die tonight you would go to heaven?

2. If you were to die tonight and God were to ask you, "Why should I let you into My heaven?" How would you answer?

Of the evangelism training class participants, more than 90 percent of them answered yes to the first question, which is a simple question asking them, "Are you saved?"

To my surprise, many of them answered the second question, expressing their righteousness to me, as follows: "I am a good honest person, I prayed a Sinner's Prayer, I've done many good deeds, I have important ministry position in my church, I am very religious, I've been blessed spiritually and materially, I've been teaching Sunday school for many years, our family has a long history of serving Him, I sing in our church choir, I am very consistent in my giving tithes and offerings, I have many spiritual gifts and experiences, and so on."

I knew the first question presented a serious problem, as everyone expected to answer yes or no. The problem is that this question asks us to declare our salvation story as finished. If we answer yes, then there is no continuation of the salvation story.

After realizing that there was a serious problem with this question, I started praying to the Lord for a solution. As always, the Lord did not delay and quickly answered this evangelist's earnest prayer.

The Lord guided us to create the following questionnaire, which increased from two to five questions, and we made it possible to choose the best answer for each question.

Question 1: If you die tonight, how certain are you that you will enjoy eternal life with God in heaven?

( ) Not quite sure ( ) 50 percent ( ) 75 percent ( ) 90 percent ( ) 100 percent

Question 2: If God asks, "With what qualifications do you enter the kingdom of heaven?" What would your answer be?

Question 3: Do you feel that the forgiveness of sins has not been fully resolved in your heart, and are you still worried about your sins?

( ) Yes ( ) No ( ) Not quite sure

Question 4: Even after receiving the forgiveness of sins through the atonement of Jesus Christ, are you worried that you will lose your salvation if you continue to commit sins because your body is weak?

( ) Yes ( ) No ( ) Not quite sure

Question 5: To how many people have you witnessed the Gospel in the past thirty days?

( ) 0 or 1 ( ) 2 or more ( ) 5 to 10 ( ) more than 10

We made an interesting but shocking observation. Even evangelism training class participants who checked 100 percent in question 1 and answered no to questions 2, 3, and 4, still seemed to struggle with question 5, asking, "To how many people have you witnessed the Gospel in the past thirty days?"

On average, almost 98 percent checked "0" for the number of people they've witnessed to during the past thirty days.

Shocking Reality: Almost All Believers Do Not Evangelize!

They have no interest in the Lord's earnest words to bear witness to the Gospel. The saints are not interested in God's earnest request and God's wishes; instead, they ask God to grant their wishes and blessings.

They do not and cannot enjoy the abundant blessings God promised that the saints receive when they evangelize, and they disobey the command to share in the sufferings of the Lord while preaching the Gospel. They have never been able to evangelize; they do not live according to God's will; they do not know the essence of the resurrection; they do not have the heart of God for the expansion of God's kingdom; they shed not a single drop of tears or sweat to spread the Gospel.

The Bible speaks clearly. Realize evangelism accurately, and live the rest of your life as an evangelist with whom God is very pleased. The Bible tells us that evangelism is inevitable, as it is our mission.

Many saints like to ask for blessings, but when the Bible says there will be woe, they hate it, ignore it, and feel bad. What the Bible says is not just about listening to good things. The Bible clearly says that if you do not evangelize, woe will come.

The apostle Paul preached the Gospel to many people, saved many souls, and established many churches, and he was not ashamed before God because he did what he had to do. On the other hand, if we do not continue the work of witnessing the Gospel, God's woe will come to us.

A brief paraphrase of 1 Corinthians 9:16 could read, "Will you just obey, or will you be beaten and reluctantly obey?"

> For if I do this thing willingly, I have a reward: but if against my will, a dispensation of the gospel is committed unto me. (1 Corinthians 9:17)

This verse says that if you preach the Gospel joyfully with a willing and glad heart, God will reward you.

After all, evangelism is our mission that we must do, but instead of waiting until the crisis of life comes, God says that if we do it voluntarily, a reward will be given.

In the structure of the Bible, many commands and blessings are repeated. The best summary is Proverbs 3. "Do it, and I will bless you," God says. Why does God command us to "go" 1,514 times throughout the Bible?

God promises to bless us when we obey His commands. Yet the saints are not interested and simply refuse to obey. In order to be blessed, we all must obey the Word of God. The Bible says that salvation comes through faith, but blessings come through obedience to the Word of God. No matter how long you go to church, if you do not obey, you will not be blessed. The repetition of commands and blessings is the structure of the entire Bible.

What is my reward then? Verily that, when I preach the gospel, I may make the gospel of Christ without charge, that I abuse not my power in the gospel. (1 Corinthians 9:18)

In verse 16, Paul says that evangelism is an unavoidable task, and in verse 17, he says that evangelism is a voluntary task. Then, in verse 18, he defines evangelism as something that must be done freely. Someone has shared the Gospel with me, so I sit here today and worship God. I pray to the Lord that this Gospel that has been passed on to me after thousands of years will be proclaimed through me, and I have the responsibility to distribute it.

Our life is short, and no one is born with a guaranteed period of life. Up until now, I have lived a life in which I have only boasted of my sins, but from now on, I am determined to live a life that preaches the Gospel that God is pleased with, likes, and desires.

One more final urgent request to you: Please examine and reconfirm your faith!

Because it is so crucially important, I want to emphasize one last time God's Word in 2 Corinthians 13:5: "Examine yourselves, whether ye be in the faith." It is really important for us believers to confirm salvation while living the faith.

If you cannot confirm your salvation, it is because you are not saved.

If you do not have the assurance of salvation, your faith will be shaken.

If your idea of being saved is constantly changing, there is no accurate proof of salvation in your heart. Through the assurance of salvation, we believers live a life of holiness and sanctification before God.

The worst life we can ever imagine on this earth will be if we turn out to be not a true born-again Christian even though we have lived our whole life as a Christian.

So Paul commands the Corinthians, "Examine yourselves, whether ye be in the faith." Are you really 100 percent saved? Endless disbelief and doubts about our own beliefs must be discouraged, but testing and confirming our beliefs is essential for us believers.

If your faith is true, you will have eternal life; if your faith is false, you will receive eternal punishment. Looking at the religious life of the saints today, it seems that they are unaware that the faith we need to check and confirm is such an important and very crucial thing. There are many people who say they believe and know Jesus Christ and God but have no interest in God's Word. There are many people in the church who are satisfied with a lukewarm religious life and proper Bible knowledge.

The apostle Paul gives the standard for this test. Test your faith and prove yourself by the standard of this test that Paul sets out in 2 Corinthians 13:5.

> Examine yourselves, whether ye be in the faith; prove your own selves. Know ye not your own selves, how that Jesus Christ is in you, except ye be reprobates? (2 Corinthians 13:5)

Are You Really and Truly Saved?

When I ask the saints this question, even among those who go to church and say that they are Christians, there are far more people who hesitate to answer this question than those who confidently answer that they have really been saved. "Yes, I go to church" is easy to answer, but very few believers say, "I am born again; I am truly saved."

One thing we Christians must never be ignorant of is the truth about our own salvation. Some people think that salvation has to be worked out for the rest of their lives. Some say you must die first to know for sure.

Asking whether a person is saved is never meant to diagnose or judge a person's salvation.

For the good Christian fellowship of faith, salvation must be proved. If he or she is new to church, it is very important to know whether he has been saved, whether he has a testimony of salvation, and whether he makes a good confession of faith. We all need to examine and prove ourselves whether we are in the faith, in Christ, saved, or born again.

God Wants All People to Be Saved

The first thing we need to know in examining salvation is that God wants all people to be saved and come to the knowledge of the truth. God does not save only those whom He has chosen and predestined, but He wants all people to be saved.

Does God want to save me? Does God delight in saving me? Of course, the answer is a resounding YES! God is pleased to save all of us, no matter who we are or what we have done.

> For this is good and acceptable in the sight of God our Saviour; who will have all men to be saved, and to come unto the knowledge of the truth. (1 Timothy 2:3–4)

Finally, reconfirm the evidence that you are truly saved through the Word.

How do I know if I am really saved? The definitive answer to this question can be summed up in two words: eternal security. If there is a certain time in your life of faith that you have received God's gift of salvation, you are forever safe. We call this biblical doctrine the eternal guarantee of salvation for the saints. The term *eternal security* means that your salvation lasts forever.

> He that believeth on the Son hath everlasting life: and he that believeth not the Son shall not see life; but the wrath of God abideth on him. (John 3:36)

The Bible promises you will have eternal life if you have the Son.

The eternal guarantee of salvation is explained by the phrase, "Once you are saved, you are always safe!" This guarantee means that you will never be punished to hell for your sins. It is impossible for you to lose that salvation. You are safe from the risk of losing your salvation.

> And this is the record, that God hath given to us eternal life, and this life is in his Son. He that hath the Son hath life; and he that hath not the Son of God hath not life. These things have I written unto you that believe on the name of the Son of God; that ye may know that ye have eternal life, and that ye may believe on the name of the Son of God. (1 John 5:11–13)

The eternal guarantee of our saints' salvation is a biblical fact from God. These are the true words of God, so you don't have to worry about your salvation, fear that the devil will take it from you, or tremble in fear that you may go to hell.

You no longer have to worry and be anxious in your life because you have surely been saved. The faithful God has given us many promises in the Bible that assure us that we are surely saved.

If you feel that God has not surely answered your prayers for salvation, take comfort in these words:

> He shall call upon me, and I will answer him: I will be with him in trouble; I will deliver him, and honour him. With long life will I satisfy him, and shew him my salvation. (Psalm 91:15–16)

The eternal guarantee of salvation is a wonderful truth that can give you the assurance that you will live only for the Lord.

What shall we say then? Shall we continue in sin, that grace may abound? God forbid. How shall we, that are dead to sin, live any longer therein? (Romans 6:1–2)

Beware! Satan Takes Advantage of Our Weak Hearts

The reason why it is difficult for us believers to accept the promise of the Bible that it is the eternal guarantee of salvation is because Satan takes advantage of our weak hearts.

In fact, it is difficult for us humans to understand fully the guarantee of eternal salvation. It is not logical for God to give such assurances when we know that we are still guilty of sin. But the Word of God is true.

We must accept it by faith, because God has said it to be true. Don't let Satan win this battle, and absolutely believe what God says. The Word that God has spoken will solve the problem. Absolutely accept the eternal security of the believer with firm faith, just as when you received the Gospel of salvation by faith.

Still too many people wonder, "How can I know for sure if I am really saved?"

We will show you the correct answer through the Word of God. The answer will be clearly shown by the true Scriptures. First of all, when you accept Jesus Christ as your personal Savior and Lord, you are adopted by God the Father. Just as you always have a physical parent, you always have God as a spiritual father.

For as many as are led by the Spirit of God, they are the sons of God. For ye have not received the spirit of bondage again to fear; but ye have received the Spirit of adoption, whereby we cry, Abba, Father. The Spirit itself beareth witness with our spirit, that we are the children of God: and if children, then heirs; heirs of God, and joint-heirs with Christ; if so be that we suffer with him, that we may be also glorified together. (Romans 8:14–17)

When you become a child of God, you also become a brother of Jesus Christ. You have become, with Christ, an heir to God's eternal inheritance. God has given you the authority to become His child, because you have dedicated your will to God's salvation.

Give thanks and praise God for becoming a child of God with absolute trust in the saving work of Jesus Christ!

But as many as received him, to them gave he power to become the sons of God, even to them that believe on his name. (John 1:12)

Eternal Guarantee of Your Salvation!

Your salvation begins with God the Father and continues through Jesus Christ, the Son of God. Your salvation is guaranteed because the Son personally knows you. This important fact can be fully understood through the following two Scripture passages:

My sheep hear my voice, and I know them, and they follow me: and I give unto them eternal life; and they shall never perish, neither shall any man pluck them out of my hand. My Father, which gave them me, is greater than all; and no man is able to pluck them out of my Father's hand. I and my Father are one. (John 10:27–30)

Not every one that saith unto me, Lord, Lord, shall enter into the kingdom of heaven; but he that doeth the will of my Father which is in heaven. Many will say to me in that day, Lord, Lord, have we not prophesied in thy name? and in thy name have cast out devils? and in thy name done many wonderful works? And then will I profess unto them, I never knew you: depart from me, ye that work iniquity. (Matthew 7:21–23)

If you are a saint that the Lord clearly knows, your salvation is eternal and secure.

God is not a man, that he should lie; neither the son of man, that he should repent: hath he said, and shall he not do it? or hath he spoken, and shall he not make it good? (Numbers 23:19)

The Lord is not slack concerning his promise, as some men count slackness; but is longsuffering to us-ward, not willing that any should perish, but that all should come to repentance. (2 Peter 3:9)

You are sealed by the Holy Spirit. The assurance of your eternal salvation begins with God the Father, continues through the Son, and is then sealed by the Holy Spirit. The eternal guarantee of the salvation of the saints is possible because the whole Godhead works together. God exists as one who reveals Himself as the Trinity we know as Father, Son, and Holy Spirit. Each Person of the Trinity accomplishes the complex work of carrying out the work of eternally securing your soul.

You Can Know and Be Sure That Your Salvation Is Undoubtedly Secure

These things have I written unto you that believe on the name of the Son of God; that ye may know that ye have eternal life, and that ye may believe on the name of the Son of God. (1 John 5:13)

The Bible Was Written by God

The Bible teaches the doctrine that your salvation is an eternal guarantee. The more time you spend reading the Bible, the fewer your doubts about salvation will be. If you often have doubts about your assurance of salvation and become anxious, I want to share with you the solid assurance, joy, and emotion that the Lord gives to our GO! Evangelists.

GO! Evangelists Experience the Joy of Spiritual Victory!

The seventy disciples in the Gospel of Luke experienced spiritual victory while evangelizing. They came to know the power of the name of the Lord, and they would come back with emotion and joy. They reported to the Lord this way: "Lord, even the devils are subject unto us through thy name" (Luke 10:17).

How happy and proud these disciples must have been. Think of the demons surrendering and yielding before the seventy disciples. It cannot but be exhilarating and surprising joy. The disciples experienced the joy of spiritual victory.

In this way, there is the joy of spiritual victory for those who evangelize in the name of Jesus Christ. Spiritual victory is not in my strength but in the power of the name of the Lord.

The power of the name of the Lord is the power that is picked up by the evangelists.

The Lord said to the seventy disciples who were overjoyed:

And he said unto them, I beheld Satan as lightning fall from heaven. Behold, I give unto you power to tread on serpents and scorpions, and over all the power of the enemy: and nothing shall by any means hurt you. Notwithstanding in this rejoice not, that the spirits are subject unto you; but rather rejoice, because your names are written in heaven. (Luke 10:18–20)

There Was Really Something to Be Happy About.

The evangelists were filled with the joy of spiritual victory. This joy is great.

The disciples really had something to be happy about, but they didn't know it. But the Lord taught us what we should be really happy about. Saints, we should always rejoice in the Lord.

But why should we rejoice? It is the joy we all need and deserve. It is also a spiritual joy, a very precious joy. It is a joy that must be tasted and deeply enjoyed.

Ultimately, the most valuable joy is the joy that our names are written in heaven!

"Rejoice, because your names are written in heaven" (Luke 10:20).

What does it mean to say that our names are written in heaven?

It clearly means that we are saved. We have become children of God. It is the fact that we are not children of darkness but children of light. What we should rejoice in the most is that we have been saved from the destruction of eternal death and have gained eternal life.

Ladies and gentlemen, the greatest joy among joys is the joy of salvation.

There is no greater joy than the joy of salvation.

He that overcometh, the same shall be clothed in white raiment; and I will not blot out his name out of the book of life, but I will confess his name before my Father, and before his angels. (Revelation 3:5)

There is a reward prepared by the Lord for those whose names are written in the book of life.

But without faith it is impossible to please him: for he that cometh to God must believe that he is, and that he is a rewarder of them that diligently seek him. (Hebrews 11:6)

His lord said unto him, Well done, thou good and faithful servant: thou hast been faithful over a few things, I will make thee ruler over many things: enter thou into the joy of thy lord. . . . His lord said unto him, Well done, good and faithful servant; thou hast been faithful over a few things, I will make thee ruler over many things: enter thou into the joy of thy lord. (Matthew 25:21, 23)

Is Your Name Written in the Book of Life?

Have you ever thought about how happy and thrilled you would be if the Lord said, "Your name is written in the book of life" while we live on this earth? Did you know that among the saints in the New Testament, there were saints who actually heard this amazing word?

The first case was the seventy disciples in the Gospel of Luke who went on a missionary tour. To the disciples who returned from their missionary journey, the Lord clearly said, "Your names are written in the book of life." These are the words the Lord personally spoke to them while they were still all alive on this earth.

The second case was in the Book of Philippians. The apostle Paul said, "The names of my co-workers are in the book of life."

These co-workers were saints living on this earth at that time.

And I intreat thee also, true yokefellow, help those women which laboured with me in the gospel, with Clement also, and with other my fellowlabourers, whose names are in the book of life. (Philippians 4:3)

In these words, we can know the secret of the names of the Philippians written in the book of life through the relationship between the apostle Paul and the Philippians.

This is because the apostle Paul, who became a true shepherd, devoted his life to pastoring so that the names of the Philippians could be recorded in the book of life.

The Philippians were yoked together with the apostle Paul and worked hard for the Gospel. They were the members of the church who obeyed God's word of love with him for the witness of the Gospel. The apostle Paul called them, "my joy and crown" (Philippians 4:1).

> But none of these things move me, neither count I my life dear unto myself, so that I might finish my course with joy, and the ministry, which I have received of the Lord Jesus, to testify the gospel of the grace of God. (Acts 20:24)

Another Class of People Whose Names Are in the Book of Life

Another class of people established by the Lord, like the apostle Paul, are GO! Evangelists who are now giving their lives to bear the yoke and work hard for the Gospel to save so many perishing souls of all ethnic groups.

These are the evangelists the Lord recognizes and to whom He confirms, "Your names are written in the book of life." These GO! Evangelists are believers who have been planting the seeds of the Gospel for several years already by thousands to tens of thousands.

In my personal experience, I started this evangelism ministry and began to experience the wonderful grace of God by planting the seeds of the Gospel in thousands of souls.

It was when the number of people I personally met and planted the seeds of the Gospel in exceeded several thousand. When I was filled with the joy and enthusiasm of witnessing the Gospel one day, I suddenly started seeing too many unsaved souls around me, and the great anxiety and unstoppable pain for them began to overwhelm me.

As I was witnessing the Gospel, tears suddenly began to flow from my eyes. Then I found myself crying uncontrollably and praying to my Father. "Heavenly Father, I'm so sorry. While I was planting the seeds of the Gospel, I never really imagined there would be so many unsaved souls. God, how long have You been hurt?" I kept crying and asked the Lord again. "Lord, in this American land where there are many Christians, even if I sweat and testify for the Gospel for several days, why don't I meet the Christians who testify of the Gospel like this?"

The Lord made me realize that if there is only the joy and emotion of salvation and no sorrow for the countless souls who have not been saved, that is not what the Lord is pleased with as a Christian. The Holy Spirit who dwells in us gives sorrow for the many unsaved souls as much as we rejoice because of the grace of the Gospel.

We GO! Evangelists realize God's deep sorrow for lost souls first, and He lets us feel and experience God's excruciating pain and sorrow for those perishing souls.

After planting several thousands of Gospel seeds, I suddenly realized that I had surely crossed a river of grace from which I could never return.

At this moment, I was truly experiencing the deep grace of God, and I had no hesitation and absolutely no doubt in my faith. I could confirm that I was truly living as one who is surely saved, whose name is written in the book of life.

Now, among the many GO! Evangelists in the United States, all the saints who plant the seeds of the Gospel and evangelize with the joy and excitement of God are living the life of an evangelist with the confidence and assurance that their names are written in the book of life. This is the assurance, thrill, joy, and faith that God gives.

The River of Grace GO! Evangelists Crossed

Do you saints remember? The Lord said to His disciples, "Do not rejoice that the demons surrender to you, but rejoice that your names are written in heaven."

Remember also the words of the apostle Paul, who said, "Truly help my fellow co-workers with my yoke, whose names are in the book of life."

Who can assure us that the names of our GO! Evangelists are written in the book of life? To our evangelists who have already crossed the river of grace, the Lord has led them to possess that confidence without any doubt because He spoke with confidence by the inspiration of the Holy Spirit. GO! Evangelists have already crossed the river of grace with absolutely no return!

We GO! Evangelists now long for the glory of God on a higher level, and what we all long for and look forward to is the day when we will stand before the judgment seat of Christ.

For we must all appear before the judgment seat of Christ; that every one may receive the things done in his body, according to that he hath done, whether it be good or bad. (2 Corinthians 5:10)

Judgment and Reward for What You Have Done, Good or Evil

All, without exception, will stand before the judgment seat of Christ. And you will be rewarded and rebuked according to what you have done in your body, good or bad.

You should know that there are two books in heaven. One is the book of life, and the other is the book of works.

Those whose names are recorded in the book of life will enjoy the kingdom of God in glory forever in heaven after the second coming of the Lord. On the other hand, those who are not written in the book of life will be thrown into hellfire and will be punished forever in a flame that cannot be quenched or burned.

The book of works records all people's good and evil deeds. On the day when Jesus returns to judge the world, everyone must confess with their own lips their deeds. It is truly terrifying and trembling to have to say everything written in the book of works with one's own mouth.

John said, "And the books were opened: and another book was opened, which is the book of life" (Revelation 20:12). God will have three books that will be opened at the Great White Throne judgment, and those that stand in that judgment, according to the revelation of the apostle John, will be judged by those things that are written therein.

Everyone Will Stand before the Judgment Seat of Christ

The Bible speaks of three major judgments:

1. Judgment for the distinction between sheep and goats

2. Judgment seat of Christ

3. Great White Throne judgment

The judgment for the distinction between sheep and goats is a judgment that separates those who will be saved from those who will be punished in hell, according to whether or not they are written in the book of life. The judgment seat of Christ means that those who believed in Jesus will be rewarded and rebuked according to what they did in the body, whether good or evil.

What is crystal clear is that everyone will stand before the judgment seat of Christ.

So how should we live until that day comes? We must live with the awareness that how we live in our perishable bodies will determine our eternal life.

We should all be able to reminisce and confess stories that have been the joy and glory of the Lord. It should be a place to reminisce and confess stories that will please us as well as the Lord.

Hearing all our confessions, the Lord, with a bright smile on His face, will descend from the throne and embrace us, saying:

Well done, good and faithful servant; thou hast been faithful over a few things, I will make thee ruler over many things: enter thou into the joy of thy lord. (Matthew 25:23)

You must be able to stand in the place of glory and emotion that we've been all waiting for. In this glorious place, if we can stand and rejoice with the countless souls saved through our evangelism efforts, there will be no greater joy and emotion in this world.

How Old Is Your Spiritual Age?

Moses prayed to God as follows: "Teach us to number our days, that we may apply our heart unto wisdom" (Psalm 90:12). If we count the past days according to the calendar, it is very easy to count because a day is a day and a year is a year. If we count all the days we live in this world with the eyes of God, there will be days that are counted and days that are totally wasted and not counted at all.

Dear brothers and sisters, what is your spiritual age?

All people are getting older—perhaps you are thirty, forty, fifty, or sixty, seventy, eighty years old. In comparison, your spiritual age may be only a few months or years. Your spiritual age begins the day you were born again. The very day you were saved by the Lord is the day your spiritual history begins. However, even if several years have passed since you believed in the Lord, your spiritual age is not necessarily growing by a year.

Even if ten years have passed since you believed in the Lord, in God's eyes you may be a Christian less than few months old. This is because the days that God does not acknowledge are days wasted in God's eyes that cannot be counted.

As we go through life, we may not think much of our lost days. But you shouldn't console yourself that those lost days were never too many. On the day we stand before the judgment seat of Christ, we will realize and deeply regret how precious was the time we wasted.

Have you thought of the many souls who would have been saved through you in that precious time lost? During that long period of time, you should have known God more deeply and more intimately and dedicated your precious time to God with greater passion.

All of us saints must be true and faithful Christians every day. If we foolishly do not live a life that pleases God but live our lives according to our own will, it is a waste of precious time and it is very regrettable.

Starting today, we earnestly hope that we will not spend days in vain. Let us abandon everything pertaining to the flesh and live a dedicated life that fully pleases the Lord.

At this point in time, we must count how many years we have lived in vain and how much time we have left. If we live like this, waiting for the day the Lord comes, we will live the rest of our lives pleasing to the Lord.

Do You Know for Sure If Your Experiences of God Are Real?

Jonathan Edwards was one of America's greatest philosophers and theologians. His famous sermon, "Sinners in the Hands of an Angry God," is regarded as one of the most amazing revival moments in history. It can also be said that it is the best example of his sermons about hell.

This sermon was preached in the village of Enfield, near Northampton, Massachusetts, on July 8, 1741, when the First Great Awakening was in full swing. The text of the sermon was a short part of Deuteronomy 32:35 ("Their foot shall slide in due time").

The main theme of this sermon is that only God's will holds the wicked from falling into hell at any time. Jonathan Edwards expressed God's wrath and judgment on sinners, the seriousness of their danger, and the devastation of hell. At that time, many believers who listened to this sermon confessed in contrition and cried out loud, so the preacher could not continue the sermon.

Even in this day and age, the growth cessation or decrease of church membership in churches across the country tells us that there is a very serious problem in the pulpit of the church. Currently, numerous churches across the country are facing practical and secular challenges to overcome the limitations of church growth, so they attract audiences to the church by encouraging faith in blessing, material success, growth first, positive thinking, and prosperity Gospel theology.

In our pulpits in this era, only the messages of blessing, comfort, and hope that the audience likes are heard, and the sermons about the judgment of sin or the wrath of God that our faithful servants shouted in the past are drying up. I wonder if the sermon that makes us truly see our sin appears when the Holy Spirit is working most hotly.

This preacher, Jonathan Edwards, handed down the death sentence, saying that unless God stopped judgment and restrained Satan and evil with His mercy and love, all people would fall into the burning brimstone fire right now and forever.

It is only God's justice that awaits all sinners. This justice of God is the message that all sinners must hear. God will surely judge, and even though all of us sinners are trampled under the feet of God's judgment and suffer tremendous curses and suffering under the terrifying wrath of the infinite God forever, God is righteous.

All of us, at this very hour, must test and prove whether our salvation is really safe.

We all have to look back and react sensitively to our sins, to prove whether we are really safe from the terrible judgment of hellfire.

The Gospel that we evangelists proclaim is not by begging and compromise, but by faith.

The more we all do before it is too late, to relentlessly bring the countless lost souls to the realization of the terrible judgment and wrath of God, the more valuable their salvation will be.

At your age, what is your ministry given by the Lord that you must realize and jump up and run to?

Do you now understand why the apostle Paul ran for the soul salvation ministry?

> But none of these things move me, neither count I my life dear unto myself, so that I might finish my course with joy, and the ministry, which I have received of the Lord Jesus, to testify the gospel of the grace of God. (Acts 20:24)

Beloved saints, never forget the important fact that with the Lord one day is like a thousand years and a thousand years are like one day. The Lord is not late in keeping His promise, as some think He is. The Lord is patient with you, waiting for all to repent and be saved rather than for any to perish. But the day of the Lord will come suddenly like a thief to millions of unsaved people.

> For a thousand years in thy sight are but as yesterday when it is past, and as a watch in the night. (Psalm 90:4)

The only reason God has been waiting and enduring this long is because He wants all people living on this earth to never perish forever because of their ungodly life. He wants to bring all to repentance.

> But, beloved, be not ignorant of this one thing, that one day is with the Lord as a thousand years, and a thousand years as one day. The Lord is not slack concerning his promise, as some men count slackness; but is longsuffering to us-ward, not willing that any should perish, but that all should come to repentance.

But the day of the Lord will come as a thief in the night; in the which the heavens shall pass away with a great noise, and the elements shall melt with fervent heat, the earth also and the works that are therein shall be burned up. (2 Peter 3:8–10)

In the end, sooner or later, God's kindness and waiting will suddenly come to an end, and the day of the Lord, when Jesus Christ will come to this earth again, will come like a thief. This is the story of Peter, but it is also the word of Jesus Christ. For the day of the Lord has already been prepared, but it will come suddenly and unexpectedly, like a thief, to these unbelieving and unsaved people.

All the signs of this world in which we live now tell us that the Lord's return in the air is very near. Nevertheless, do you feel that the coming of the Lord is delayed? If so, you should be grateful. The reason why today has been given to you is because it gives you a precious opportunity to go to God, repent, be forgiven, and live a life of a believer whom God is pleased with as a faithful believer who has been saved from now on.

On the day the Lord returns, all unsaved people will go straight to hell.

How many people around you should hear the Gospel of salvation through you, be saved, and become citizens of heaven?

Through the inspiration and words of the Holy Spirit, all the people around you who have not yet been saved can become heavenly citizens, receive salvation just like you, and become mature citizens of heaven who plant the seeds of the Gospel whom God is very pleased with. Here again, I will tell you the secret of the blessing step by step.

1. Everyone has to experience being born again.

> Jesus answered and said unto him, Verily, verily, I say unto thee, Except a man be born again, he cannot see the kingdom of God. . . . Jesus answered, Verily, verily, I say unto thee, Except a man be born of water and of the Spirit, he cannot enter into the kingdom of God. (John 3:3, 5)

The following Scripture passages tell us exactly how to be born again and receive the Holy Spirit.

> Then Peter said unto them, Repent, and be baptized every one of you in the name of Jesus Christ for the remission of sins, and ye shall receive the gift of the Holy Ghost. (Acts 2:38)

> I am crucified with Christ: nevertheless I live; yet not I, but Christ liveth in me: and the life which I now live in the flesh I live by the faith of the Son of God, who loved me, and gave himself for me. (Galatians 2:20)

2. As a child of God, you must clearly realize the mission the Lord gives you.

> For though I preach the gospel, I have nothing to glory of: for necessity is laid upon me; yea, woe is unto me, if I preach not the gospel! For if I do this thing willingly, I have a reward: but if against my will, a dispensation of the gospel is committed unto me. (1 Corinthians 9:16–17)

And he said unto them, Go ye into all the world, and preach the gospel to every creature. (Mark 16:15)

Then said Jesus to them again, Peace be unto you: as my Father hath sent me, even so send I you. (John 20:21)

I charge thee therefore before God, and the Lord Jesus Christ, who shall judge the quick and the dead at his appearing and his kingdom; preach the word; be instant in season, out of season; reprove, rebuke, exhort with all longsuffering and doctrine. (2 Timothy 4:1–2)

But hath in due times manifested his word through preaching, which is committed unto me according to the commandment of God our Saviour. (Titus 1:3)

In the meantime, all the believers have felt the burden of evangelism, but they have lived a very lethargic life of faith with severe hesitancy and fear of witnessing the Gospel, unable to engage in spiritual warfare at all. Although all the saints want to testify the Gospel to unbelievers, they could not come forward because of fear and rejection when they testify the Gospel.

There was pity from the Lord for these countless unsaved souls, but the reality was that there were very few saints willing to obey and go and testify of the Gospel. The blessing that the Lord gave to all the saints who eagerly wanted to evangelize was GO! Evangelism to plant the seeds of the Gospel in order to readily solve this difficult problem.

3. All mature evangelists live as believers longing for and waiting for the glorious day when they will be praised as good and faithful servants before the judgment seat of Christ.

The blessings of the Lord prepared for all the saints who fulfill this mission of witnessing the Gospel were unimaginably great and amazing. GO! Evangelism is not done by our own wisdom, strength, ability, or will, but by the power of the Holy Spirit, and God makes all evangelists realize that the blessings of being filled with the Holy Spirit will come upon them.

Even at this moment, the miraculous work of evangelists planting seeds of the Gospel to hundreds to thousands of lost souls every month continues on the streets of many cities across the United States. The great and amazing blessing that the Lord bestows on countless evangelists is that they are longing for and waiting for the Lord, who will soon come down in the air. They are longing for the glorious day when they will stand before the judgment seat of Christ, and they are passionately planting the seeds of the Gospel.

> His lord said unto him, Well done, thou good and faithful servant: thou hast been faithful over a few things, I will make thee ruler over many things: enter thou into the joy of thy lord. (Matthew 25:21)

> And, behold, I come quickly; and my reward is with me, to give every man according as his work shall be. (Revelation 22:12)

Chapter 10: Your Utmost Devotion for His Highest Glory

Are you determined to be absolutely and entirely for Him and Him alone?

According to my earnest expectation and my hope, that in nothing I shall be ashamed, but that with all boldness, as always, so now also Christ shall be magnified in my body, whether it be by life, or by death. (Philippians 1:20)

The only thing that non-believers and born-again Christians have in common is that they are in the same space. The dreams of the people of the world are limited to this world. The success they want are dreams that come true only while living on this earth. However, the dreams of Christians do not stop on this earth but extend into eternity.

Born-again Christians are people who know for sure why they have to live through the mission given by Christ. They are people who know why you have to work hard in business, why you have to study hard, and why you shouldn't be lazy. It is because they know that their lives are directly related to eternity and that they are related to the glory of Jesus Christ. But non-believers don't know why they have to live.

But none of these things move me, neither count I my life dear unto myself, so that I might finish my course with joy, and the ministry, which I have received of the

Lord Jesus, to testify the gospel of the grace of God. (Acts 20:24)

The grand dreams of the people of the world aimed for living happily and becoming famous on this earth. It's amazing to see people in the world trying to succeed. There is no one who eats everything, sleeps all the time, and succeeds. They think it's these things are their happiness and the true meaning of life, but when they think about their destiny, it is not a true dream (Matthew 25:41). However, the dream that a Christian has is a true dream and truly remains.

Then shall the King say unto them on his right hand, Come, ye blessed of my Father, inherit the kingdom prepared for you from the foundation of the world. (Matthew 25:34)

The Christian life is not focused on self but on the glory of the Lord. If our dream is simply to eat, sleep, and enjoy life, it is a dead dream. Since the Christian life is related to eternity, our life plan is not limited to longevity.

The world is becoming more and more morally corrupt. This is because the world is dominated by Satan, the father of lies. But Christians must be different. People in the world live very hard, competitive life. However, we Christians should live harder than them, because we live a true life. Only Christians have real and eternal dreams. No matter what your dreams become in this world, I hope you will definitely become a person who gives the highest glory to God.

No matter what the apostle Paul did, he thought only of exalting the Lord in his body.

When Paul wrote to the Philippians, what he was eagerly expecting now was not release from prison. It was about not being ashamed of anything. It was about being completely bold. What Paul ultimately hoped for was for Jesus Christ to be honored through his body under any circumstances.

Whether he lived or died, either free or in prison, as long as Jesus was honored, it didn't matter what happened to him.

How did Paul have such an unwavering aim? How could Paul love Jesus Christ like this? Since Paul was always ready to die, he was also ready to live. And he was able to live a valuable and meaningful life on earth because he had the certainty of eternal life and because he had a firm goal in his life. Is Jesus being honored through the bodies of us evangelists? Are we really living well, as God had intended?

I sincerely hope you live the rest of your life as an evangelist who saves lost souls and with whom the Lord is most pleased. Whatever you do while you are on this earth, do it as to the Lord and to the glory of the Lord. God will be glorified when you have a dream and fulfill the ministry of saving countless lost souls while glorifying God through your loving evangelism.

It Is Time for a Reality Check

Suppose that you have read this book deeply and, moved by the Holy Spirit, have made a decision to live a life of a Gospel witness that pleases the Lord from now on. You secure the seeds of the Gospel, go out on the streets, and plant the seeds of the Gospel to one hundred people you meet for the first time. How many Christians do you think you can meet?

According to my personal experiences during the past few years and the testimonies of numerous GO! Evangelists, among the people who have met and been evangelized in many cities in the United States, the percentage of people who are thought to have received salvation is seriously low. On average, only one or two out of a hundred people are responding positively to the Gospel evidence.

Ladies and gentlemen, a more serious and regrettable experience is the fact that there have been cases where I have met nearly a thousand people and testified of the Gospel, but there have been cases where no one has been saved.

Rather, it is a sad reality that many people were angry with this evangelist for no reason and took a hostile attitude, saying, "I am not interested in the Gospel you are preaching at all, and I am going to a separate place." It is immediately evident that it is Satan who hates the proclamation of the Gospel the most.

The Bible says that "all that will live godly in Christ Jesus shall suffer persecution" (2 Timothy 3:12). God wants the evangelist to endure being harassed unjustly, and He has also promised compensation.

> But I say unto you, Love your enemies, bless them that curse you, do good to them that hate you, and pray for them which despitefully use you, and persecute you. (Matthew 5:44)

The Lord's Deep Groaning

Our Lord's deep yearning for Jerusalem is now His lamentation for His people who will soon be thoroughly destroyed.

Do you remember? The prophet Jeremiah lamented while looking forward to the miserable discipline and suffering of his own people. There were no tears in his eyes. Even though he was shunned by his own people and suffered persecution, he did not resent them; rather, he lamented their foolishness and stubbornness, and he prayed to God. This image of Jeremiah is also a foreshadowing of our Lord Jesus Christ.

Our Lord also loved Jerusalem very much. The deeper the affection, the deeper the sorrow. Jerusalem was on the verge of complete destruction by the will of God the Father. Jesus Christ tried to gather the people of Jerusalem together like a hen gathers her chicks under her wings, but they refused.

O Jerusalem, Jerusalem, thou that killest the prophets, and stonest them which are sent unto thee, how often would I have gathered thy children together, even as a hen gathereth her chickens under her wings, and ye would not! Behold, your house is left unto you desolate. For I say unto you, Ye shall not see me henceforth, till ye shall say, Blessed is he that cometh in the name of the Lord. (Matthew 23:37–39)

The Lord's deep groaning is because of the sins of mankind. Because of our sins, the Lord's life was one full of sorrow and tears. This love of the Lord has given us Christians living in these last days the mission of witnessing the Gospel, and now

He wants us to testify to the Gospel of salvation to countless lost souls before the door of heaven closes.

The Lord wants all the saints to plant the seeds of the Gospel in countless perishing souls with the mission of witnessing the Gospel given to us, entrusting their salvation only to God's power.

Reexamine whether your faith is full of faith that pleases God.

When you do the final confirmation of your faith using the following guidelines, you will be greatly and mightily used for the expansion of His kingdom at this end times.

1. Are you sure you are in the faith?

Examine yourselves, whether ye be in the faith; prove your own selves. Know ye not your own selves, how that Jesus Christ is in you, except ye be reprobates? (2 Corinthians 13:5)

In the text, Paul commands us to "examine yourselves" and "prove your own selves." Here we are faced with one clear fact. We are not only able to test and prove ourselves, but we are also commanded to do so.

What we need to check is, "Are we in the faith?" This is not something that can be checked by someone else, but it is something that we ourselves can check and know for ourselves. The present tense verb emphasizes the fact that we need to check and confirm over and over again.

True faith guarantees eternal salvation. However, whether or not we are in that true faith should always be the subject of testing and confirmation.

If there is a truly pitiful person on this earth, it would be one who lives as a Christian all his life but is not truly saved and is going to hell. You don't even want to imagine your life could be this kind of life.

A sure proof that Jesus is in you is your love for Jesus Christ. Your love for Jesus Christ must bear fruit through obedience. Therefore, the way to be sure that Jesus is in you is to confirm how much you obey the Word of God and whether you are living the life of an evangelist toward the lost souls, as the Lord earnestly asks you to.

Are you a person of true faith?

Is Jesus Christ in you?

Do you really love Jesus Christ?

Do you promise to live a life as an evangelist, planting the seeds of the Gospel to countless lost souls, as the Lord has earnestly requested and commanded?

These are the questions Christians should ask themselves every day.

This is the Gospel that must be preached every day.

2. Have you been born again?

This is one of life's most important questions. Jesus Christ said:

Verily, verily, I say unto thee, Except a man be born again, he cannot see the kingdom of God. (John 3:3)

Verily, verily, I say unto thee, Except a man be born of water and of the Spirit, he cannot enter into the kingdom of God. (John 3:5)

Jesus finished the teaching by reminding Nicodemus that those who choose to be reborn and follow God will come into the light, able to live righteously while looking forward to their eternal reward.

And this is the condemnation, that light is come into the world, and men loved darkness rather than light, because their deeds were evil. For every one that doeth evil hateth the light, neither cometh to the light, lest his deeds should be reproved. But he that doeth truth cometh to the light, that his deeds may be made manifest, that they are wrought in God. (John 3:19–21)

The most important and crucial thing in Christianity is being born again.

However, it is true that not everyone who goes to church is born again.

You can go to church, attend worship services, serve, participate in all church activities, work, and receive positions.

It is true that unless you are born again by the Holy Spirit, you are no different from an unbeliever. Christianity is a religion of faith that lives by receiving the life of God.

Jesus tells Nicodemus three times that man must be born again of the Holy Spirit. So why did He say that he had to be born again?

Everyone in this world received Adam's blood and was conceived in sin and born as a sinner (Romans 5:12, 17, 19).

Because of his disobedience, sin entered the world, and through sin death came to all men. Because you have this sin in yourself, you have no choice but to go to hell and die twice.

But God provided a way of salvation for all sinners. It is to accept the life of God before leaving this world. This is the work of being born again by the Holy Spirit.

3. Have you received the mission that Jesus gives you, and are you living the life of an active and enthusiastic evangelist?

But none of these things move me, neither count I my life dear unto myself, so that I might finish my course with joy, and the ministry, which I have received of the Lord Jesus, to testify the gospel of the grace of God. (Acts 20:24)

The mission that God has given us is to generously offer the Gospel of salvation of Jesus Christ to countless perishing souls.

And he said unto them, Go ye into all the world, and preach the gospel to every creature. (Mark 16:15)

God wants the world to know that He is the source of all our needs. It is His mission for the world to believe in His Son and become Christian. God sent His beloved Son to save us and make us know that all our needs are met in Christ.

For though I preach the gospel, I have nothing to glory of: for necessity is laid upon me; yea, woe is unto me, if I preach not the gospel! For if I do this thing willingly, I have a reward: but if against my will, a dispensation of the gospel is committed unto me. (1 Corinthians 9:16–17)

4. Do you long for the day when you will be praised as a good and faithful servant before the Lord?

His lord said unto him, Well done, good and faithful servant; thou hast been faithful over a few things, I will make thee ruler over many things: enter thou into the joy of thy lord. (Matthew 25:23)

All of us Christians ultimately seek the joy of our Master. We live as Christians because we enjoy His pleasure. We are loyal to our work to please the Lord. Regardless of how many talents are given to me, if it makes the Lord happy, I will be loyal to His work.

5. Are you earnestly waiting for the Lord who is about to descend in the air, and are you diligently witnessing the Gospel to countless lost souls?

I charge thee therefore before God, and the Lord Jesus Christ, who shall judge the quick and the dead at his appearing and his kingdom; preach the word; be instant in season, out of season; reprove, rebuke, exhort with all longsuffering and doctrine. (2 Timothy 4:1–2)

Please think about Paul's situation during this passage. Paul worked tirelessly for over thirty years. He preached the Gospel wherever he went and devoted himself to serving the church with all his strength. But at the time he wrote this passage, he was facing death in prison. Paul knew that he would soon die. In this passage, Paul was giving his last words to Timothy. He was writing this so that the important command would be delivered well before his death, explaining to him the purpose of life and what to live for.

What makes these words especially solemn for us is the fact that we, too, will one day stand before God when the time is right. We, too, will stand before the Lord who will judge. The Lord will appear. At that time, He will judge the living and the dead and establish His kingdom. Our Lord comes again as a judge to establish and rule the nation. This fact sets our life goals right and makes a difference in our lives. We are all waiting for the Lord to come again, and when the time comes, the Lord will settle our lives.

Paul, looking forward to the day when he would meet the Lord before his death, exhorts not only himself but also Timothy and all those who follow the Lord to look forward to that day and live. When we clearly remember that one day we will stand before the Lord, we ask ourselves, "What do we live for?" Paul's words to Timothy are the correct answer to the question.

Listen to Paul's words. Paul solemnly delivered the command that gives us the answer to our lives. The command we must set as our goal in life and engrave in our hearts is found in verse 2. There are five commands in verse 2, and the key is the first command. Paul begins verse 2 with this command: "Preach."

The reason for the command is given in verses 3 and 4. Why should we urgently spread the word? Because the time is coming. Paul warns Timothy in advance of what will happen to him. In fact, at this time, he is telling Timothy about the future, but as Paul wrote of the last days in chapter 3, we can see that Timothy is already living in this time. And this time will continue until the Lord comes again.

What is a Christian's greatest success? It is how much you obeyed the great command of the Lord rather than hoarding a lot of wealth, knowledge, and power.

Therefore, everyone, the greatest task in the world is to save souls. The greatest miracle in the world is that a sinner believes in Jesus and his soul is saved, and the most rewarding thing in the world is to save his soul. The most valuable accomplishment in the world is to save the soul. The most beautiful feet in the world are the steps to save souls, the most beautiful words are to believe in Jesus and be saved, and the most valuable time is spent to save souls. The most valuable service is saving souls. The most urgent thing is to save the soul.

To those who evangelize to many perishing souls, God gives them great blessings and rewards in this world and in the world to come, and He makes them shine forever.

Please keep in mind that all of us who have been saved are now the missionaries of the Gospel testimony that the Lord wants, and we emphasize this important fact to all the saints around us and urge them to live as evangelists.

The following Bible passages emphasize the fact that all of us who have been saved are established as witnesses of the Gospel.

The Spirit itself beareth witness with our spirit, that we are the children of God: and if children, then heirs; heirs of God, and joint-heirs with Christ; if so be that we suffer with him, that we may be also glorified together. (Romans 8:16–17)

But hath in due times manifested his word through preaching, which is committed unto me according to the commandment of God our Saviour. (Titus 1:3)

For though I preach the gospel, I have nothing to glory of: for necessity is laid upon me; yea, woe is unto me, if I preach not the gospel! For if I do this thing willingly, I have a reward: but if against my will, a dispensation of the gospel is committed unto me. (1 Corinthians 9:16–17)

I have planted, Apollos watered; but God gave the increase. So then neither is he that planteth any thing, neither he that watereth; but God that giveth the increase. Now he that planteth and he that watereth are one: and every man shall receive his own reward according to his own labour. (1 Corinthians 3:6–8)

But none of these things move me, neither count I my life dear unto myself, so that I might finish my course with joy, and the ministry, which I have received of the Lord Jesus, to testify the gospel of the grace of God. (Acts 20:24)

And, behold, I come quickly; and my reward is with me, to give every man according as his work shall be. (Revelation 22:12)

The Bible emphasizes evangelism, the Great Commission of Jesus Christ, so that there is no room for excuses. In a world where it is not easy even for myself to live by the Word of God, preaching the Gospel to others and making disciples of Christ requires great dedication and hard work. God speaks accurately about evangelism through the Word, and He wants us to live as evangelists whose lives please God.

Even though we know that evangelism is the mission and task of Christians, the reason why most Christians are helpless is because of secular opportunism, pluralism, and trends in the digital age. However, since it is God's command, we must obey it. If you go out and plant the seeds of the Gospel, you will enjoy the joy and thrill of heaven given by God and the blessing of being awakened spiritually.

I urge you in the name of the Lord to be comforted and strengthened by the following words about the difficulties and persecutions you will experience while longing for and waiting for the glory of heaven and testifying the Gospel on this earth.

Blessed are ye, when men shall revile you, and persecute you, and shall say all manner of evil against you falsely, for my sake. Rejoice, and be exceeding glad: for great is your reward in heaven: for so persecuted they the prophets which were before you. (Matthew 5:11–12)

Blessed are ye, when men shall hate you, and when they shall separate you from their company, and shall reproach you, and cast out your name as evil, for the Son of man's sake. Rejoice ye in that day, and leap for joy: for, behold, your reward is great in heaven: for in the like manner did their fathers unto the prophets. (Luke 6:22–23)

The secret of the most successful and blessed GO! Evangelist is to be able to truly say, "I am His, and He is accomplishing His work and His purposes through me."

And, behold, I come quickly; and my reward is with me, to give every man according as his work shall be. (Revelation 22:12)

Are You Ready for the Rapture? Be Ready for His Imminent Return!

At the Rapture, all believers will meet the Lord in the air at the trumpet call of God.

The Rapture: Our Blessed Hope!

The Christian's "blessed hope," referred to in Titus 2:13, is the imminent, personal return of our Lord Jesus Christ. The word *hope* in the New Testament implies "a joyful and confident expectation," based upon the promise of our Lord Himself (see John 14:3).

Are You Rapture Ready?

This is the day when Jesus Christ will come down from heaven to snatch His church who have been born again of the Spirit of God. This Rapture event is the hope we have. All believers, whether dead or alive, who belong to Christ will meet the Lord in the air at the trumpet call of God.

Watch, therefore, and be ready! Our blessed hope is the promise of the Rapture (Titus 2:13)!

Biblical Evidence for the Imminence of the Rapture

All it takes is the following three passages:

Let not your heart be troubled: ye believe in God, believe also in me. In my Father's house are many mansions: if it were not so, I would have told you. I go to prepare a place for you. And if I go and prepare a place for you, I will come again, and receive you unto myself; that where I am, there ye may be also. (John 14:1–3)

For the Lord himself shall descend from heaven with a shout, with the voice of the archangel, and with the trump of God: and the dead in Christ shall rise first: then we which are alive and remain shall be caught up together with them in the clouds, to meet the Lord in the air: and so shall we ever be with the Lord. (1 Thessalonians 4:16–17)

Behold, I shew you a mystery; We shall not all sleep, but we shall all be changed, in a moment, in the twinkling of an eye, at the last trump: for the trumpet shall sound, and the dead shall be raised incorruptible, and we shall be changed. (1 Corinthians 15:51–52)

The author of *The Second Coming of Jesus*, Oscar Lory, wrote in his book:

The Second Coming of Christ is mentioned over 300 times in the New Testament. On average, one in every 25 verses from Matthew to Revelation speaks of the Second Coming of Jesus. There are more than 3,000 direct prophecies of Jesus' second coming throughout the Old and New Testaments. And it is said indirectly more than 1,000 times in the entire Bible. If we have spoken once about redemption, we have spoken twice about the Second Coming. If the first coming of Jesus was mentioned once, he talked about the second coming eight times. . . . If we judge the importance of doctrine on the basis of what is most prominent in the Bible, the second coming of the Lord stands above all and no less than any other matter. The greatest event of this world history is the return of the Lord Jesus Christ. Therefore, when considering the second coming, the greatest of great events, it is not surprising that much of the Scriptures are devoted to it.

There are more than three hundred prophecies in the Old Testament regarding the first coming of Jesus, and all of them have been fulfilled. And while most of the biblical prophecies have already been fulfilled, some remain to be fulfilled at the Second Coming.

The Difference between the Rapture and the Second Coming

The topic of Bible prophecy and the end times is indeed quite an interesting one.

The sequence of events spoken of in the Bible is as follows: the Rapture, the tribulation, the Second Coming of Christ, the millennial kingdom, and the new heaven and new earth.

Revelation 21–22 give us a detailed picture of the new heaven and new earth. After the end of this world, the present heaven and earth will disappear and be replaced by a new heaven and a new earth. The eternal dwelling place of believers will be the new earth. The new earth is the heaven where we will live forever. It is in this new earth that the new Jerusalem, the heavenly city, will be located. There will be pearl gates and golden roads over this new land.

Heaven (the new earth) is the physical place where we will dwell with glorified bodies (1 Corinthians 15:35–58). The heaven believers will experience will be a new and perfect planet on which we will dwell. There will be no sin, no evil, no sickness, no pain, and no death in the new earth.

However, the ultimate gift of the Gospel is not the splendid new heaven and new earth itself. The ultimate good of the Gospel is not even a redeemed body. The ultimate good of the Gospel is neither forgiveness, nor redemption, nor propitiation, nor justification. These are all means to an ultimate end.

The ultimate good of the Gospel, which makes it truly good news, without which all other gifts cannot be good news, is God Himself. The best thing about heaven is that our Lord and Savior will be with us (1 John 3:2). We will come face-to-face with the Lamb of God, who loved us and sacrificed Himself so that we could enjoy heaven and be with Him there forever.

What If I Miss the Rapture?

Many Christians will be shocked and won't be able to believe that they have been left behind. Many churches are not teaching and urging them to prepare for the Rapture. Words about the Rapture, the end times, and the tribulation are rarely mentioned in their sermons.

For this reason, the Christians left behind will turn against the pastors and the leaders of the church with great fury and hold them accountable.

The Rapture will completely separate those who knew and followed the Lord in spirit and truth from those who only knew the Lord through tradition and formality. The whole world will see who is a true Christian and who is a false Christian!

> Not every one that saith unto me, Lord, Lord, shall enter into the kingdom of heaven; but he that doeth the will of my Father which is in heaven. Many will say to me in that day, Lord, Lord, have we not prophesied in thy name? and in thy name have cast out devils? and in thy name done many wonderful works? And then will I profess unto them, I never knew you: depart from me, ye that work iniquity. (Matthew 7:21–23)

After the trumpet call, it will be too late to repent. At that time, many people will mourn and ask the Lord with regret. But all of that will be in vain. The Lord has already said over and over again that only those who have lived a prepared holy life can enter. All those people not raptured will unfortunately go through the great tribulation!

Regarding the great tribulation, Jesus spoke: "Then shall be great tribulation, such as was not since the beginning of the world to this time, no, nor ever shall be" (Matthew 24:21). The great tribulation is a time of terrible persecution. Jesus said, "Then shall they deliver you up to be afflicted, and shall kill you: and ye shall be hated of all nations for my name's sake" (Matthew 24:9) This is the time of the fall, as Jesus said wickedness will increase and love will grow cold (Matthew 24:12).

The whole world will be thrown into chaos. The demons that were bound will come up from the earth (Revelation 9:2). Everyone will be looking out for themselves only. The great tribulation must be avoided by all at all costs. Those who want to prepare for Jesus must put Jesus first in everything in their lives. You should never put anything else before Jesus. We must remember the words recorded in Hebrews 12: "Holiness, without which no man shall see the Lord" (Hebrews 12:14).

The words of Jesus in Matthew 5:20 are rarely mentioned from the church pulpit. It means that if our righteousness is not better than that of the Pharisees and scribes, we cannot enter the kingdom of heaven. God's Word clearly says that entering the kingdom of God is difficult. If you are a man of worldly, lukewarm faith, you are not ready (Revelation 3:16)! Remember the five foolish virgins. If your lamp is not filled with oil or does not shine the light, you are not ready (Matthew 25:1–13)! If you have lost the taste of salt and live like so many other people in the world, you are not ready (Matthew 5:13)!

Very soon, millions of people shall suddenly disappear, and there will be mass panic, widespread fear, and devastation.

What will happen to all the missing people—your loved ones and the children? All non-Christians and those who pose as Christians who miss the rapture will then be left behind to suffer through the tribulation—a-seven year period of catastrophic pandemonium and earthquakes, terrible plagues, and bloodshed.

When the church is gone, there will be no one there to pray for you and support you.

If you don't have the guts to stand up and proclaim that you now accept Jesus Christ as your Lord, do you really think you will have enough courage to do that after the Holy Spirit and all Christians have been removed from this earth?

Don't bet your soul that you will even have that chance or the courage to do so. Many faithful Christians do not believe you will even have a chance to be saved during the great tribulation.

Your chance is now! If you are going to be saved, you must accept Jesus Christ as your Lord and Savior NOW!

If you are not ready yet, please go back to the previous chapters of this book and get fully prepared by placing your faith and trust in God alone.

And, behold, I come quickly; and my reward is with me, to give every man according as his work shall be. (Revelation 22:12)

Index

F

H